ANTIQUITATE REGIA CONTINUA

Sophy Lécoa

Hereditas evolvitur,
unum volumen ad tempus.

A legacy unrolled, one volume at a time.

BORN TO

BREAK THE SPELL

A Whisper from Back Then

Sophy Le'coa

Published by Whisperlight Publishing

ISBN: 978-1-969457-00-5

Library of Congress Control Number: 9781969457005

Cover design: Sophy Le'coa
Interior artwork and scroll designs: Sophy Le'coa

Printed in the United States of America

DISCLAMER

This is a work of nonfiction memoir. While the events are por-
trayed as accurately as possible, some names and identifying details have been changed to protect the privacy of individuals. Any
resemblance to persons, living or dead, in instances where names
have been altered, is purely coincidental.

Dedication

To my Mama —
a powerful soul who shaped mine.

There are loves that hold you softly…
and loves that hold you so firmly
you grow strong without even knowing it.
Mama, you were both.

You taught me strength wrapped in discipline,
and discipline wrapped in love.
You gave me lessons that I clung to,
and lessons I vowed to carry differently —
yet always toward the same goodness
you wanted for me.

Even your rare moments of tenderness
were like drops of diamonds —
precious, unrepeatable,
and cherished to infinity.

You never let go of me.
Not when the days were heavy,
nor when the miles were many.
You are the heartbeat of our family,
a force of nature,
and the hero I am endlessly blessed to call mine.

And if all I had in this world was you, Mama,
I would still have everything.

— Sophy Lecoa

Acknowledgments

"To my first reader — my beloved daughter. You walked every page with me before the world did, laughed and cried with my words, and reminded me that my story is not only mine, but ours."

To every soul whose path has crossed mine, in ways seen or unseen — thank you.

Some of you I have known and loved, others I have never met. Yet your presence has reached me through the lives you've touched, the choices you've made, and the ripples you've set in motion.

We are all one story — billions of moments and lives, woven together into something far greater than ourselves.

This book is one thread in that vast, shared tapestry, and I am deeply grateful to be part of it with you.

—Sophy Lecoa

When Silence Had a Name

There are stories that slip quietly into your life…
and there are stories that stand at your door, knock hard, and refuse to leave until you open.

This is one of those stories.

I was born into a world wrapped in silence — a place where words were measured, dreams were dangerous, and even the air seemed to carry secrets. But inside that silence lived a heartbeat… and that heartbeat was mine. It carried whispers of hope, flashes of rebellion, and an unshakable belief that somewhere beyond the gray, there were colors waiting for me.

What you'll find in these pages is not just my childhood. It's the laughter that escaped in forbidden places, the tears that carved me into who I am, and the tiny sparks that grew into a fire no one could put out. It's the people — some who held me softly, some who held me firmly — each one shaping the girl who would one day chase the American Dream.

I have written this for you — not just to read, but to feel. Because in every step I took, I believe there is a step you will recognize. In every locked door I faced, there is one you may have faced too.

So take my hand. Walk with me through winters of scarcity and summers of wonder. Listen to the voices I wasn't supposed to hear. Stand with me in the quiet moments that changed everything.

And perhaps, by the time we reach the last page, you'll find pieces of your own story here... and a reminder that no matter how gray the world may seem, the colors are always there, waiting.

Because this is not just the story of my girlhood — it is a journey through the iron grip of Communist Romania, where freedom was a distant dream...
until one day, it wasn't.

Table of Contents

Chapter 1

Golden Echoes

The first memory I carry from childhood rests in a quiet evening that feels as though it belonged to another world.

Daddy was stretched out on the sofa, his body heavy with the weariness of a long day's work. Clara and I sat cross-legged on the rug, competing to see who could pick up more *jazz* (lint-dust) from the carpet — one of Daddy's little games to keep us busy while he stole a moment of peace.

Clara was delicate, with hair like pale wheat and a face that seemed to hold its own quiet light.
Her green eyes, flecked with amber, had a calm depth, as if guarding a secret never spoken.
Even her hands, with their long, graceful fingers, carried a fragile elegance.
She was like a living work of art — graceful, mysterious, and softly watching over us like a small light in the home.

I was the youngest — not just in our house, but in the whole family.
Dark-chestnut hair, big curious eyes, cheeks made for

pinching —

to everyone, I was the bold one, the cheerful meddler,
always ready to laugh loud, ask questions, and leap into the
story.

When Mama dressed me in something new,
I twirled like a little queen, inviting everyone's gaze.

If Clara was quiet grace,
I was the playful spark —
always ready to turn the smallest moment into a celebration.
Together, we completed each other,
while the world outside kept its rhythm to the song of our
evenings.

In the background, the television hummed its familiar
lullaby, ending the *Telejurnal* (news) transmission with that
unmistakable tone I can still hear echoing in my mind to this
day.

I glanced at Daddy. He had dozed off, the weight of the
day finally pulling him under. I signaled to Clara, who
pressed a finger to her lips and gestured for me to follow her
into the other room.

But I didn't want to leave.
I wanted to play with Daddy.

So, I tiptoed back, leaned close, and pinched his eyelashes gently, lifting each eyelid one by one.

"Boo!" he roared suddenly, making me jump out of my
skin.

He burst into laughter — deep, joyful, unstoppable —
at the look on my startled face. In a flash, he scooped me up,

his arms strong and warm, and tickled me until my little belly hurt from laughing.

From that day on, it became our ritual — our game of love and delight. A Daddy–Sophy moment, carved forever into my heart.

I remember *Noapte bună, copii!* (Romanian cartoon — "Good Night, Children!") with Mihaela coming on the TV, and how I would bounce and clap with happiness every single time.

"Clara, quick!" I'd call, urging her to watch with me.

But the cartoon was always too short — far too short for my little heart that wanted joy to last forever.

Clara loved to tease me, pretending to "predict" its ending.
"It's almost over," she'd say.
"One, two, three… aaand done!"

"Nooo!" I'd cry, desperate for just one more moment.

She'd promise not to do it again… but she always did. And every time, I believed her. Looking back now, it makes me laugh. But back then, it broke my tiny heart — because in my mind, Clara was the one who stopped the cartoons.

And then there was Mama…

Her soft beauty, perfectly painted red nails. Her tender hugs that felt like lullabies even before she spoke. I remember our naps together — the three of us curled under one blanket — while Daddy gently closed the bedroom door to keep the sound of his laundry from disturbing us.

The world was small then. But it was whole. And we needed nothing more.

Some days we'd go on family picnics, baskets full of food and voices full of laughter. The air felt different out there — freer, brighter, the kind of brightness that only exists when you're too young to worry about anything except running barefoot through grass. My little cousins would gather us all for their "big performance" — my cousin plucking her mandolin to impress the adults. Everyone clapped and cheered as if it were the grandest stage in Romania.

On the way home from daycare, Daddy and I would stop by the big shop window filled with dolls. I'd press my nose to the glass, pointing out my favorites, and he'd nod seriously, as if committing their faces to memory for the day he could buy one.

Sometimes, he'd stop for sunflower seeds, slipping a handful into his jacket pocket. I would help myself — eating them whole, shells and all — proud to be "just like Daddy," even though they scraped my throat. He'd laugh, patting my head, and I felt like I'd passed some secret grown-up test.

Other days, our stop was for a beer for him, a *Citro* or *Fruco* for me, and a bowl of peanuts to share between the four of us at home.

And oh, the teasing when Mama found out. "Sophy, come to Mama. Tell me — where have you two been?" she'd say, narrowing her eyes with mock suspicion. "We didn't go to the restaurant, Mama," I'd insist. "I've seen you on TV," she'd counter. "Tell me the truth." "Okay… just a little," I'd confess, and Daddy would burst into laughter.

"You said you wouldn't tell, Sophy!"
"But Daddy… the TV…" I'd protest — and they would both laugh so hard my little heart felt ready to burst from the happiness of it all.

There were four chairs at our dinner table, and in those early days, every one of them was filled. Daddy sat across from Mama, making sure the fish on my plate had no bones. With careful fingers, he rolled the soft white meat into a ball, pressed it into the warm *mămăligă* (polenta), touched it to *mujdei* (garlicky sauce), and placed it into my already open mouth.

While I chewed, he was already preparing the second bite. And just as he was about to give it to me, I would announce, "I need to go to the bathroom," making everyone groan and laugh at once.

I was captivated by everything about him.

Sometimes, sitting on his lap during dinner, I'd trace the face of his watch with my tiny finger, watching the shiny hand skip from point to point as if it had all the time in the world. I breathed in the warm, steady scent of his cologne, loved the way his stubbly cheek brushed against mine, tickling until I squealed with delight — my laughter always answered by his smile, the one that felt like it belonged to me alone.

After dinner, he would take a *Mărășești* (Romanian brand tobacco) cigarette from his golden *tabachera* (cigarette case) embossed with the insignia of the Romanian flag, and step out to the balcony. I would wait for him to return — his coffee cup still on the table, steam curling into the dim light.

When he came back, he would sit again to finish it, newspaper spread open before him. I didn't care for the newspaper — gray, lifeless, full of ugly pictures. My whole world was his lap, his watch, his scent, and the gentle thrum of his presence.

From another room, Clara's squeaky violin floated in, Mama's soft laugh slipping between the notes as she encouraged her to keep playing.

It was a small apartment, but those evenings made it feel like the center of the universe — four chairs, four hearts, one world entire. I didn't know then how quickly such worlds can change.

Even now, when I think back to those days — the laughter, the scent of clean laundry, the warmth of Mama's voice, Daddy's pocket full of sunflower seeds, the clink of glasses, the glow of shared peanuts in a bowl — I feel as though God placed a piece of heaven in my childhood.

A treasure of innocence, glowing softly in my memory. Fragments of pure gold from another life.

A life without worries.

Without fear.

Without pretending.

A life that ended sharply, suddenly — the day everything changed, dividing time forever into before and after.

~ ~ ~ ~ ~ ✧ ~ ~ ~ ~ ~

What Life Whispered to Me

Some memories feel too tender to belong to this world.
They drift through time like pieces of a dream I once
lived — or maybe borrowed from another life.

I hold them close because they are proof
that innocence existed once,
that laughter came easy,
that love had a home.

And yet… even as I cherish them,
I often wonder what if?

What if that wholeness had lasted longer?
What if those evenings — the tickles, the picnics, the
teasing over peanuts —
had been the rule, not the exception?

Life doesn't answer.
It only whispers this:

Treasure the fragments of heaven you were given,
because sometimes,
they are all that remain of a world that could have
been.

— Sophy Le'coa

**CHILDREN ARE BORN
TO WONDER —
RULES, LOGIC AND FEAR
ARE LEARNED LATER.**

Sophy Lécoa

Chapter 2

The Longest Sleep

There was still a place for him at the table.
Four chairs, just as before. Mama sat at her end, Clara beside
her, me across, and the empty seat at the head — Daddy's seat
— waiting like a held breath.

No one said it out loud, but I kept glancing at it as if, at
any moment, he might step in from the hallway, smelling
faintly of cologne and cold air, shaking off his coat, smiling
like the world had decided to be kind again.

I imagined the sound of his shoes — that particular
rhythm — crossing the tiles. The way his hands would rest
briefly on the back of his chair before sitting down. I imagined
the warmth of his palm, guiding the fish bones away from my
plate like he always did, rolling the soft meat into a ball,
dipping it in *mujdei* and placing it gently in my mouth. I could
almost taste the garlic and the salt of his attention.

But the chair stayed still. Silent.

I didn't know that the next memory I would carry would feel like winter breaking into my summer — cold, sudden, and impossible to forget.

It was Christmas Eve, 1977. I was three years old — wrapped in a world too small to understand sorrow, yet already heavy with something unspoken.

The table shimmered like a dream: red-and-white napkins folded neatly at every plate, crystal glasses waiting to be filled. The air was alive with the smell of brownies and steaming *sarmăluțe* (cabbage rolls), a warmth that promised joy.

The old pick-up player sang *muzică populară* (country music) in gentle crackles, my tiny feet skipping across the floor, clapping in rhythm, my eyes fixed on the treasure beneath the tree — four oranges, glistening as if dusted with gold.

"Where's Daddy?" I asked, my voice a bubble of hope. "He'll be right back," Mama said, her hands flying from dish to dish, cheeks flushed with heat and hurry, her eyes shining with something I couldn't name.

Sleep came suddenly — heavy as a winter blanket. My last memory was Mama's face: blurred, hurried, beautiful… before everything slipped into darkness.

When morning came, the world had changed. Something was missing. Something I couldn't name. And though I was too young to grasp it, a quiet line had been drawn that night — a line that would forever split my life into before and after.

Later, I learned the truth. Daddy had been crossing the street when a car hit him head-on at the pedestrian crossing. They rushed him to the hospital, but they couldn't even tell Mama until morning — they hadn't known who he was. Mama waited all night.

In silence.

Only when the sun rose did the truth reach her. I can't imagine what she felt in those hours. But I know this: in front of us, she didn't fall apart. She didn't cry. She didn't scream. She stood there — quiet, unshaken — like a pillar in the middle of a mute storm.

The next thing I remember is waiting at daycare, expecting Daddy to pick me up. But that day, my Aunt M. came instead.

On the walk home, the cold air bit at my cheeks, and I did what I always did with Daddy: I stopped at the *Librărie* window (Romanian shop with books and some toys), staring at the dolls lined up on the other side of the glass. They looked beautiful, lit by the pale winter sun, their eyes sparkling as if they were watching me back.

I stayed there a long time — longer than usual. My aunt didn't pull me away. She let me stand there as long as I wanted. And for a moment, that felt good. I didn't yet know why I needed that kindness.

When we reached home, the stairwell was filled with the scent of damp coats and candle wax. People were everywhere — their breath visible in the chilly air, their voices low, their faces strange. Heavy. Quiet.

From the bottom of the building up to our door — all eyes turned to me as I passed. Their silence followed me like a shiver.

Inside, the line continued, winding through our hallway… all the way into the living room.

And there — there was Daddy.

My heart leapt with joy.

He had come home!

He was here!

He was lying down, flowers all around him. The air smelled of lilies, cold air, and the faint trace of tobacco. He looked peaceful. Too peaceful.

Aunt M. passed me gently to Mama's hand. I slipped my hand from Mama's grasp and ran to him.

I knew just what to do — the way I always woke him when we played: pinching his eyelashes, lifting them open, waiting for the laughter to burst into the room and bring everything back to life.

But Mama pulled me back, softly, carefully.

"Leave Daddy now," she whispered. "He's very tired. He needs to sleep."

I didn't understand.

I looked at her — her face pale and strange — and at Clara, standing silent, staring at the floor.

Something felt wrong.

Cold. Unreal.

Like a bad dream I couldn't shake.

But I thought I could fix it.

Me and Daddy could fix everything.

If I could just try again…

This time, Mama held me tighter.

"Let him sleep this time, Sophy," she said, her voice breaking just enough for me to feel it. *"Please… let him sleep."*

In that moment, my little heart understood something that words could not.

Something had ended — and it would never be fixed.

Years later, on another Christmas Eve, Mama told me softly:

"There's no greater irony than this.

Your father died, hit by a car…

and we had been saving every penny to buy one.

In the end, we used the money to bury him."

I didn't know then how long grief could stay — how it could change shape, soften, and yet still find ways to surprise you years later.

~ ~ ~ ~ ~ ✧ ~ ~ ~ ~ ~

What Life Whispered to Me

Some moments never leave you.
They live inside your chest like a shadow,
like a soft bruise you can't rub away.

I was too small to understand death that day —
but my soul understood loss.

I learned that silence can be louder than any scream.
That grief can stand upright,
wearing Mama's face,
holding a child's hand.

That life can draw an unthinkable line

in an instant —
turning before into a place you can never go back to.

And sometimes, love does not get a goodbye.
It just lingers in a room full of flowers,
waiting for you to wake someone who never

wakes again.

From that day on, the dinner table felt different.
Four chairs had once been filled with the

warmth of us —
Daddy making sure my fish had no bones,
shaping each bite with polenta and garlic sauce,
my mouth open in anticipation of the next.

Now one sat empty.
It would not be the last time.

— Sophy Le'coa

~ ~ ~ ~ ~ ✧ ~ ~ ~ ~ ~

LIFE IS A FRAGILE DASH
BETWEEN TWO ETERNITIES
—
BEFORE BIRTH
AND
AFTER DEATH.

Sophy Lécoa

Chapter 3

One Dream Left, Another Born

The house looked the same, yet everything inside it had shifted.

The chairs sat where they always had. The kitchen clock ticked at the same pace. But the air had changed — heavy, hollow, as if a piece of it had been taken away and no one knew how to put it back. Even the light coming through the curtains seemed different, as though it carried less warmth.

Mama's hugs were still soft, still warm, but they felt like stolen fragments. Her stories were shorter now, spoken in half-breaths between long silences. At night, I would watch her hands moving across the kitchen table — folding napkins, peeling potatoes — and feel something I couldn't name. It was as though she was somewhere else entirely, carrying a weight too heavy to share with me. The hum of the refrigerator, the faint tick of the clock, and the sound of her knife against the cutting board became the background to my childhood.

evenings — small, steady sounds that made the silence in her voice even louder.

Clara filled the spaces Daddy once held.
She ran between rooms like a whirlwind — bossy and loud one moment, my fierce protector the next. Whenever kids tried to pick on me in the yard, Clara would step forward like a tiny soldier, chin high and eyes blazing. But her love came with rules, and I learned them quickly.

Before, I had run to Mama with every complaint about Clara's orders, expecting her to step in and make things "fair." But now, those little betrayals ended with a sister's scolding — quick, sharp, whispered so no one else could hear. It didn't wound me the way I thought it might. Instead, it taught me. I learned silence. I learned obedience. Not out of fear, but because I began to see: Clara wasn't trying to be cruel. She was standing where Daddy once stood — a child herself, yet somehow already my shield.

The Walks That Changed
Even the walk home from daycare was different now.

When Daddy picked me up, we lingered. We stopped at the *Librărie* window, my breath fogging the glass as I stared at the dolls lined up inside. Sometimes, he would buy sunflower seeds, slipping the warm packet into his jacket pocket so I could reach in and grab a handful. Peanut shells in my pocket — the salt stinging my lips, the rough edges scraping my throat, but tasting like happiness.

18

Other days, we'd stop at the little restaurant for our *Fruc*-and-peanuts ritual, sharing a glass bottle of soda and a bowl of salted peanuts as if it were a royal feast. The clink of the bottle against the glass and the crack of peanut shells under our fingers are sounds that still live in my memory like treasures wrapped in gold paper.

With Mama, it was different.

Her steps were quick, her grip on my hand firm. No seeds. No dolls. No stopping. The walk became the straightest possible line between daycare and home, as if even a single pause was a luxury she could no longer afford. Her eyes stayed fixed forward, her jaw set — not unkind, but unreachable. I think now she was afraid that if she stopped moving, she might never start again.

The Vanishing

The visits stopped, too.

Before, weekends had been alive with the laughter of uncles and aunts, the clink of coffee cups in the kitchen, the smell of something sweet baking in the oven. My little cousins would perform for us, their tiny fingers plucking mandolin strings, the notes buzzing like happy bees through the air. There had been teasing back and forth between Mama and Daddy — playful banter that always ended with the whole room laughing.

Now, the rooms were still.

No voices spilling from the kitchen. No music. No smell of coffee drifting lazily through the air. It was as if those people had vanished from our world overnight, carrying a piece of our joy with them. The silence left behind was larger than our small apartment, stretching into every corner like a shadow we couldn't chase away.

The Miracle Night

Saturday nights still held a fragile kind of magic. Our old black-and-white TV — the one that hissed static and sometimes spun the picture sideways — was our portal to another world. We had only one channel, and movies were rare, but oh, how we waited for them.

That night, the screen crackled and warped, and Clara gave it the usual fix — two small fists pounding it back into shape. We squealed when the image returned, grainy but alive.

And then came the miracle.
The first American movie I had ever seen.

For Romanians back then, it was as rare as finding sunlight in a locked room.

Clara laughed, clutching my arm, eyes wide as she drank in every scene. I tugged her sleeve, whispering, "What are they saying? Tell me!" She tried, tossing me quick translations at first, but her excitement got the better of her. She didn't want to miss a single second.

So I fell silent.
And I just watched.

Something in that flickering, trembling screen seemed to breathe color into our gray living room. The people in that world moved as if gravity itself loved them. They laughed as though joy wasn't rationed. They carried something invisible but unmistakable — a light I had never seen before.

I couldn't understand the words, but my little heart understood what it was seeing. Years later, I would know its name: *freedom.*

The kind our souls are born knowing.
The truth no one can erase.
The instant we glimpse it, we remember.

From that night on, I carried America in my heart — not as a place on a map, but as a dream.

Daddy had been my first dream — tender, bittersweet, tied to the past.
This dream was different. Fierce. Unshakable. A beacon on the horizon.
And nothing in the world could dim it again.

~ ~ ~ ~ ~ ✧ ~ ~ ~ ~ ~

What Life Whispered to Me

Some dreams are gifts we are handed at birth —
fragile, glowing, carried in small hands until time
takes them away.

Others strike like lightning —
a single flicker that sets the soul on fire,
a truth we didn't know we were missing
until we felt it burn inside us.

I learned that night that freedom is not a promise the
world gives.
It is a memory from heaven.

It lives in us before we have words for it.
It waits for the moment we dare to recognize it —
and once awakened,
it pulls us forward with a strength nothing can

silence.

— Sophy Le'coa

~ ~ ~ ~ ~ ✧ ~ ~ ~ ~ ~ ~

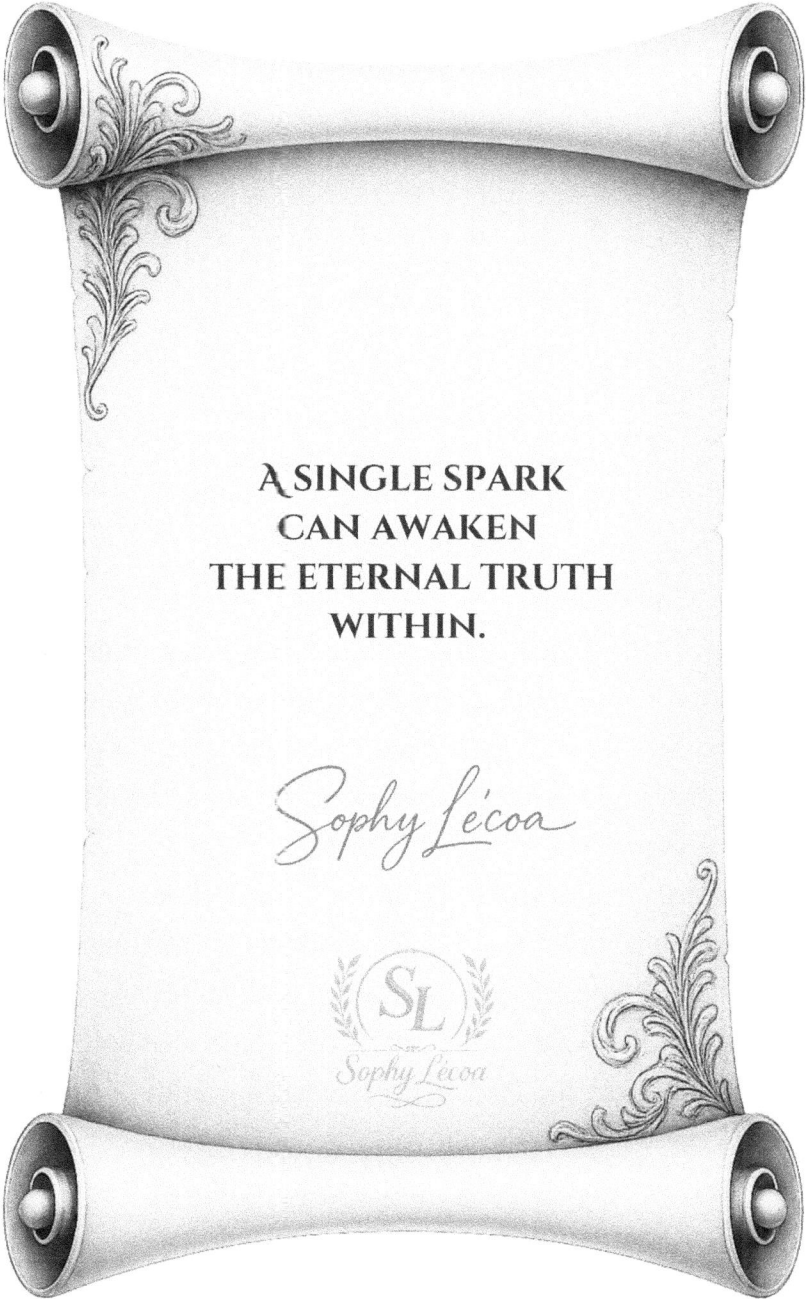

A SINGLE SPARK
CAN AWAKEN
THE ETERNAL TRUTH
WITHIN.

Sophy Lécoa

Chapter 4

The Endless Troubles

My First Clients

I have loved beauty for as long as I can remember —
anything that could be made prettier, softer, more magical.
Give me an object and a little time, and I would transform it.
And now that I had my treasure chest of ideas from American
movies, I was ready to practice in earnest.

My only doll, Luiza, became my first "client" — and, if
I'm honest, my first victim. I made clothes for her out of old
scraps, brushed and pinned her hair in endless styles,
decorated her face with "makeup" from my box of colored
pencils — the kind you had to keep warming with your
tongue so the waxy tip would smudge just right.

But that day was special. It was haircut day.
An American haircut day.

By then, I had mastered exactly two words in English:
Hello and *Sharrap* — my toddler version of shut up.
I used them with the elegance of a Hollywood starlet.

"*Hello*, Luiza," I'd say, blinking slowly, eyelashes
fluttering like a film diva. "Are you ready for a haircut?
An *American* haircut?"

Then, with my precious little scissors, I'd reassure her
in my most important tone:
"*Sharrap.* You will look better."

Hours later, Luiza sat before me completely bald.

But my passion for haircutting didn't stop there.
The carpet fringes were next.
Then the carpet itself.

It only ended when Mama stormed in, her voice sharp
enough to cut the air. I froze mid-snip, my tiny heart
thudding.

"Enough!" she said. "Or else."

For a while, I obeyed.
But scissors weren't just tools — they were temptation.

After Luiza's baldness and the carpet's "bangs," I still
needed someone to beautify. So, I turned to Clara.
While she slept.

Just a little snip. One strand, maybe two. Nothing she'd
notice. I whispered to myself:
"*Sharrap.* Just a little bit. You'll thank me later."

She never did.

But she never caught me — not until the day her
hairline shifted just enough to raise one eyebrow across the
dinner table.

Mama got involved again, this time for real. Scissors were confiscated.

But artistry cannot be banned.

If Luiza had no hair, I'd give her new hair. I threaded a needle, poked strand after strand through her hard plastic scalp until my little fingers burned and bled. Hours later, she had a full, stringy head of "hair."

I beamed at her.

"Hello, Luiza."

She said nothing.

So I added my second word.

"Sharrap. You're gonna like it."

Then I turned her around, picked up my scissors... and cut it all off again.

Because in my world, beauty always deserved a second try.

The Beauty School of Communist Romania

By the time I was five, everything became a client:

Clara's bangs (trimmed in her sleep).

My own hair (without permission).

Even a friend's cat.

Beauty had a price — and sometimes, it smelled like burnt hair.

We had no curling irons, so we used Mama's screwdriver heated on the stove. We'd wrap our hair around the hot metal and dream of movie-star curls. Sometimes it worked. Other times, there was a sizzle, followed by whole strands breaking off like burnt threads.

Then came bath night. Warm water was rationed, so Saturday evenings were the only time Mama filled the tub. She scrubbed us until our skin squeaked — and that's when the evidence floated up. Little burnt strands drifting like dark confetti, silent proof of our glamour crimes.

Mama's sugar-and-water hairspray was our other secret weapon — stolen more often than borrowed. It held curls better than anything else, though it also attracted flies.

Clara sometimes joined me, but she had a blackmail streak. If I broke something, she'd keep it over my head for days. So I learned to experiment alone.

Mama thought the problem was the scissors. She didn't know the real problem was me — too much energy, too many ideas buzzing to sit still.

The Gymnastics Takeover

When scissors were banned, my body became my outlet. I discovered gymnastics after watching Nadia Comăneci on TV. It started small — a clumsy handstand against the wall, a crooked cartwheel. But soon, I was convinced I was destined for Olympic gold.

Clara wasn't the gymnast; she was the strategist. "Not near the lamp, Sophy… try the bed."
"Careful with Mama's vase."

Most of the time, I listened. Most of the time.

One afternoon, my cartwheel clipped the lamp. Crash. Another time, my perfect flip sent me headfirst into the window frame. Crack.

My crowning moment? A triple somersault off the bed that snapped the bed frame in half.

Between my fearless leaps and Clara's safety plans, our living room survived only by miracle.

The Little Singer

My confidence soared the day Mama discovered I had a good voice. Soon, I was in the preschool folk group, wearing costumes she made herself. One — all white, shiny, and tight from neck to ankle, with puffed sleeves and a bright red scarf — made me feel like a star. Clara wanted one too, and Mama made it happen. We became a matched pair, "little celebrities" in her eyes.

Guests at home were treated to performances on command — songs, dances, recited poems. But when it came to declaring how much I loved school, I always nudged Clara to do it for me.

Then came the question no child could escape:
"And you, little one… what do you want to be when you grow up?"

One evening, something in me refused to give the approved answers.

Hands on hips, I declared:
"I'm going to be… a professional guest."

The room exploded with laughter. Everyone laughed except Mama, who studied me with quiet eyes, as if she knew there was truth in my choice.

The Day I Ran Home

Mama sometimes dropped us at Aunty Vio's. Aunty adored Clara but barely tolerated me.

"You don't help enough," she'd say.

"I'm a guest," I'd answer. "Guests don't do dishes."

In her house, the price for doing dishes was red nail polish. Clara got it. I didn't.

When the room was empty, I climbed a chair, grabbed the bottle, and painted my nails — messy, smudged, but glorious.

Aunty caught me. Her voice became a storm.

"You little devil! Worse than an animal!"

Each word was a slap. My small chest tightened until I could hardly breathe.

I slipped to the door. The handle was cold.
And then I ran.

I boarded the number 5 bus, switched to the number 8, and whispered all the way, *"Home… to… Mama."*

When I burst through our door, Mama's face drained to white, then she grabbed me with a hug so fierce I thought she'd never let go.

"Please, Mama… don't make me go there again," I sobbed.

Her voice shook, but her arms were steady:

"Okay, baby. You stay here with Mama."

Later, I learned the whole family had been in a panic. Maybe that was the day Mama decided she needed more "help" — the kind that made sure scares like that never happened again.

What Life Whispered to Me

There is a bravery only a child knows —
the bravery of speaking truth with a trembling voice,
of running toward love even when the world feels un-
safe.

Adults call it disobedience.
I call it courage.

I promised myself long ago never to silence the little
girl who dared to say what she wanted to be.
Never to call a child's wild heart "wrong."

What life whispered to me was this:
Stay close to the heart of a child. Protect it. Listen to
it.
Let it keep its courage.

Because in that courage lies the truest kind of wisdom
—

the kind adults often lose but desperately need to re-
member.

— Sophy Le'coa

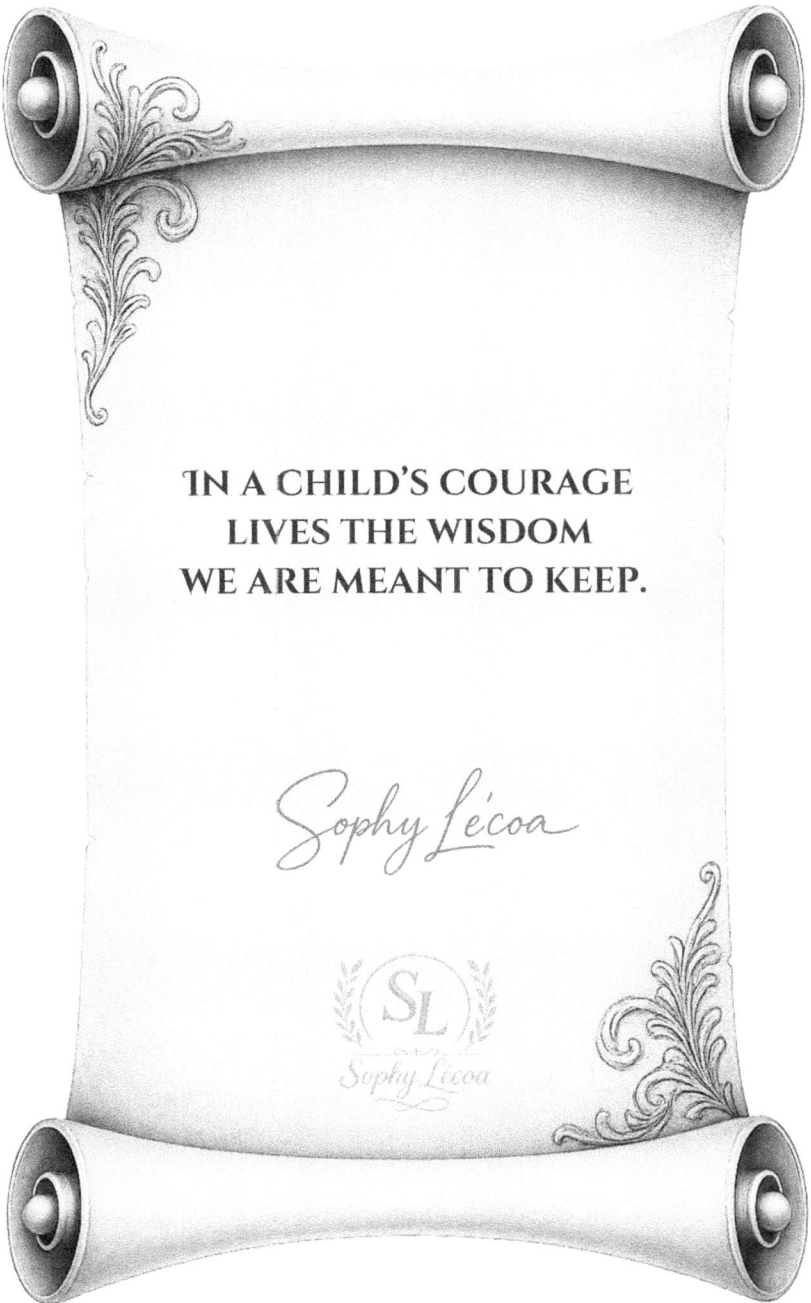

IN A CHILD'S COURAGE
LIVES THE WISDOM
WE ARE MEANT TO KEEP.

Sophy Lécoa

Chapter 5

The Promise

They don't need papers, signatures, or solemn oaths. They're made of glances and whispers, of the way your Mama's tired eyes flicker with hope when she says, "It will get easier soon." They're built from a longing so big, you almost believe you could reach out and touch it.

I remember that winter afternoon when a new kind of hope was promised to us. The grown-ups talked in fragments, their voices low but sharp, like knives cutting deals I didn't quite understand. But one thing I caught — the only thing that mattered — was this: Mama would finally have someone to help her, someone to lift the weight from her weary shoulders. Someone to give her back a little breath, a little time for us, for love.

And I believed it. Oh, how I believed it.

That promise wasn't just words. It lived in my chest, beating fast every day I pressed my nose against the icy window,

waiting for the figure who would change everything — who
would give me back the hugs that lingered and the laughter
that stayed in the room long after Mama walked in.

When footsteps finally echoed down the hallway, my
heart galloped like it knew joy was just a few breaths away.

Grandma Arrives

And then I saw her — tall, serious, wrapped in dark
clothes and a scarf that framed her face like a soldier's helmet.
Mamaia (Romanian for Grandma) clutched her bags tight, her
lips pressed thin.

I darted forward, arms open.
"Hello, *Mamaia!*" I chirped, pressing my face into her coat.

She hugged me back, but it felt… distant.
"Hello, dear," she said softly. Her voice was warm but
wrapped in fatigue.

I searched her face for a smile. She gave me one —
small, quick — and it vanished before I could hold it.

Mamaia didn't sit to rest. She set down her bags, rolled
up her sleeves, and marched to the kitchen like a soldier on a
mission.

Mama's shoulders dropped in relief. Her voice was soft
but eager:
"With *Măicuța* (Romanian for Mammy) here, I can
finally take more shifts at the hospital… it'll help us so much."

I tried to believe it. But deep down, something felt
wrong. The hugs I'd dreamed of didn't seem to be part of this
new arrangement.

That first evening, dinner smelled different — sharper, like boiled onions and vinegar. *Mamaia* moved through the kitchen like she'd lived there forever, banging pots, clattering lids, mumbling to herself.

Mama came home late, nurse's bag on her shoulder, her face pale with exhaustion. I ran to her, arms open, and for a moment, her hug was tight enough to make me think — maybe, just maybe — everything would be okay.

The Table

At dinner, I sat beside Mama, waiting for the old warmth to fill the room.

Mamaia set down four plates with quick precision. "Eat," she said, sitting last.
She said a quiet prayer. No smile. Just the clinking of spoons against chipped bowls.

I poked my food with my fork.
"Thank you, *Mamaia*," I whispered, hoping to catch her gaze.

She nodded once, already sipping soup. Across from me, Clara's greenish eyes flicked between *Mamaia* and Mama but didn't linger on me. When our eyes met, I knew she was wondering the same thing I was: why didn't it feel like help had come?

I leaned toward Mama and whispered, "Will you stay home tomorrow?"
She brushed a strand of hair from my face.
"I wish I could, *dragă*. But Mama has to work."

Mamaia's voice cut in — not unkind, but sharp enough to slice the air:

"She works so you can eat. Finish your soup."

Clara shot me a glance, her eyes sighing for her. We both lowered our heads and obeyed.

That night, Mama tucked me in, her hands smelling of hospital disinfectant instead of home. Clara climbed into bed beside me, and in the dark, I reached for her hand. No words — just the squeeze of her fingers and the unspoken promise we would hold each other through this new silence.

Cucuie & Pinky Promises

Days passed, and "help" showed its true face.

Mamaia's hands were strong — but not for holding mine. They were for pulling my hair when I was too slow or smacking my restless fingers when I couldn't stop cutting, threading, creating. My head learned the shape of her knuckles, and the little bumps she left behind — *cucuie*, Clara and I called them.

Every time the sting brought tears, Clara was there — stroking my head where *Mamaia's* rough hands had been.

One night, when Mama came home smelling of disinfectant, I whispered, "Mama… *Mamaia's* rough on us." Her eyes softened, but her voice was heavy.

"I know, little baby. Just… try to be very good. We need Grandma's help right now."

After she left, I turned to Clara.

"Will it always be like this?"

"No," she said firmly. "*Mamaia's* old. One day soon, she'll go

35

to heaven. Then we'll have peace."

"Promise?" I held out my pinky.

She hooked hers around mine, stroking my *cucuie* gently.

"Promise."

Hope was born in the dark — not because the world was kind, but because my sister promised it would be one day.

Mischief & the Legendary Plan

Kids like us didn't just wait for peace — we made our own. During *Mamaia's* naps, we would build an alarm system, rattling toys near her bed. For extra precaution, Clara *să țină de 6* (kept watch), and I was on high alert, ready to hide the forbidden evidence my little hands were crafting.

It worked well, until we got too confident.

The legendary plan, the one we laugh about even now, came on the day Clara whispered:

"Let's see how it feels to smoke a cigarette... just like Auntie V."

We had seen Auntie puff like a queen, holding her cigarette as if it made her part of some glamorous secret club. We wanted to know what that secret was.

So, while *Mamaia* napped, we tiptoed into the pantry, our hearts racing with the thrill of mischief. Clara had swiped one of the crumpled cigarettes from the golden *tabachera* Daddy used to keep. She struck a match, her hands trembling a little, and the tip flared alive like forbidden fire.

She took the first puff, coughed so hard I thought we were done for, then handed it to me:

"Your turn," she whispered, eyes watering but determined.

I hesitated for a second, then copied her, trying to look as glamorous, but the smoke scratched my throat, made me gag, and left us both coughing and laughing silently in the dim pantry air.

And that's when it happened.

The pantry door swung open with a force that made every jar shake on the shelves. We froze, wide-eyed, smoke curling between us like a guilty cloud. And there she was.

Mamaia.

Standing in the doorway, her arms crossed, her expression a storm gathering speed.

For a heartbeat, none of us moved.

I was still holding the cigarette midair.

Then, out of nowhere, *Mamaia's* hands shot out like lightning, grabbing each of us by a fistful of hair.

"Ahhh!" I yelped.

The next thing I knew, my feet were flying out from under me. We were tossed into the living room like two guilty sparrows thrown from the nest, the cigarette abandoned, smoke curling behind us.

The storm hit full force.

Mamaia's voice roared, words crashing like thunder, a mix of scolding and disbelief:

"What are you doing? Smoking?! You think you're grown women?!"

Clara stammered, standing half in front of me like my trembling bodyguard:

"We just... we just wanted to see..."

But that only made *Mamaia's* eyes blaze hotter.

The "discipline lesson" that followed was swift, loud, and unforgettable. When it was over, we sat side by side, clutching our sore heads, vowing never to so much as look at a cigarette again.

And yet, even with tears on our cheeks, I remember Clara leaning over and whispering:

"We almost made it..."

We both burst into giggles, laughing so hard we forgot the sting for a moment.

Looking back now, we laugh even harder — because only we know how carefully planned that mischief was, how badly executed it turned out, and how much love and mischief two little girls could fit into a war of silence under *Mamaia's* reign.

But one thing's for sure: between *Mamaia's* hard hands and Clara's pinky promises, childhood taught me fast that family can hurt, protect, and save you — all in the same breath.

And still, I clung to those promises — Mama's words, Clara's pinky — dreaming of a day when help would finally feel like love.

~ ~ ~ ~ ~ ✧ ~ ~ ~ ~ ~

What Life Whispered to Me

*Sometimes, the promises we hold on to as children are
not made of words,
but of longing — for love, for peace, for someone to finally notice
how small our hearts feel under the weight of grown-
up burdens.
I once believed help meant healing.
I believed that when hands arrived to lift the load,
they would also hold us close.
But I learned early that not all "help" comes soft or
kind.
Sometimes, it leaves bruises you have to hide under
your hair,
and silences you only know how to fill with a sister's
pinky promise in the dark.
Yet even then, hope found a way to stay alive —
not because life got gentler,
but because love, even in its smallest, most fragile
form,
was enough to keep us waiting for the day
when help would no longer hurt,*

and the promises we clung to
would finally feel like love.

And maybe that is what saved us:
the quiet endurance of believing love was still possi-
ble.
Even in the cracks of broken trust, we learned to wa-
ter tiny seeds of tenderness.
Those seeds became roots,
and the roots became strength —
strength that carried us toward a future where love
would not only arrive,
but stay.

— Sophy Le'coa

~ ~ ~ ~ ~ ✧ ~ ~ ~ ~ ~

NOT EVERY HAND
CAN HOLD YOUR HEART —
YET A SINGLE PROMISE
OF LOVE CAN KEEP
HOPE BREATHING.

Sophy Lécoa

Chapter 6

Treasures and Trades

By the time I was six, our home had settled into a
rhythm that felt... heavy.
Not only from the grayness pressing against the windows,
but from the weight of the air inside —
a weight you could smell.
One of the thickest scents was *Mamaia's* soap.
She'd drag a great iron cauldron into the kitchen,
fill it with chunks of fat, pale bones, and sharp caustic flakes,
then let it boil for hours until sour steam curled around her
headscarf
and crawled into every corner of our apartment.
It clung to the curtains.
To the walls.
To our hair and clothes.

As if something had died in that pot
and refused to leave.

When the mixture cooled, *Mamaia* would slice the thick,
chalky slabs
and stack them neatly on a wooden board.
Those big, uneven pieces became our shampoo, our dish soap,
our laundry powder —
anything that needed to be washed.

I learned early that in our world,
clean didn't mean gentle.
It meant the sting in your nose,
fingers cracked open at the knuckles,
skin rubbed raw until you smelled like sorrow tangled with
soap.

But there was another scent — rarer, softer — that
sometimes slipped through the door.
It was Mama, home from a long shift at the hospital,
her nurse's bag slung over one shoulder,
bringing with her the little treasures grateful patients pressed
into her hands:
meat, sugar, cooking oil, repair services,
and — most prized of all — treats.

In Communist Romania, money alone wasn't enough to
buy what you needed.
Once your monthly rations were gone, the only way to get
more
was to trade "gifts" — cigarettes, perfumed soaps, fine coffee,
sometimes even whole pigs — offered especially to people in
higher positions.

Mama's treasures were modest compared to that,
but they kept us afloat.
Survival, folded neatly between linens in her closet.

And sometimes, among the bartered goods,
there was something just for us —
Chinese chocolate wrapped in shiny foil,
a stick of cinnamon gum that looked like magic itself.

We'd rush to her as if she were air itself,
clinging to her legs, searching her face for that secret smile.

"Guess what I brought today?" she'd tease.
"Chinese chocolate!" Clara and I would shout — every single
time.
"I don't know…" she'd pretend,
drawing the moment out like a magician before the reveal.
"Maybe you should look in my purse."

We'd dive into her bag like pirates after treasure.
She'd break the bar cleanly in half,
place a piece in each of our hands,
and watch how we closed our eyes,
letting the sweetness melt slow on our tongues
like a promise we couldn't yet name.

It tasted like +++*freedom*+++.
And we didn't even know what freedom truly was.

Most other days, we had *Gumela* —
a Romanian stick of gum so dry you could hear it crack
before collapsing into something between wet cardboard and
regret.

Our everyday chocolate was just as joyless —
a bitter slab wrapped in washed-out paper that read simply

Ciocolata (Chocolate),
as if the word itself had been stripped of color.

But whenever Mama whispered, *"Look in my purse,"*
it felt as though the whole outside world had cracked open,
and something bright and impossible had slipped through.
And Mama — tired, radiant — had caught it just for her girls.

That was the air I breathed the year I first went to
school —
a mix of soap, rationed food,
and the rare sweetness of Chinese chocolate.

And when my first day finally came,
it brought nothing new with it.

Not my uniform — already worn thin from years of
wash and wear.
Not my books — their covers soft at the edges,
their first pages faintly haunted by the erased names of
children before me.

Even my teacher wasn't new.
He was Clara's old teacher — the one Mama swore was the
best in the school.
I'd heard about him often:
how he was the kind of teacher every parent wanted.

But I wasn't sure I wanted him.
He was famous for his *"high standards"* —
which, in those days, meant more than keeping up with your
homework.

If you stumbled,
if you made too many mistakes,
you'd feel the sharp sting of his wooden pointer on your

backside —

the same stick he used to trace rivers on maps

or underline chalkboard notes.

They called him *the teacher with the pointer.*

And every child in that school knew exactly what that meant.

I hoped I would love him, just as Clara once did.

But deep down, a quiet unease stirred —

a sense that his ways would never fit the softness I longed for

in a teacher.

Even before stepping into his classroom,

I knew my heart was bracing for something it might not welcome.

~ ~ ~ ~ ~ ✧ ~ ~ ~ ~ ~

What Life Whispered to Me

When you grow up in a world where everyone is
equally deprived,
you don't call it deprivation.
You call it normal.

You think life is meant to be lived in small, rationed
breaths.
You measure joy in crumbs,
and believe a single square of chocolate
is the size of happiness itself.

You don't yet realize the row austerity —
only that the air feels thin,
and you've learned to live with low breathing.

But somewhere, without knowing it,
your soul remembers there's more.
It waits, patient and silent,
for the day you taste it…
and recognize it as freedom.

— Sophy Le'coa

~ ~ ~ ~ ~ ✧ ~ ~ ~ ~ ~

EQUALITY UNDER
COMMUNISM
IS NEVER PROSPERITY —
ONLY MISERY
EVENLY SHARED.

Sophy Lécoa

Chapter 7

The First Day and Cat Umbrella

I remember my very first day of school.
It was a rainy September fifteenth — the national day when
every child in Romania marched into a new school year.

Mama had prepared my uniform the night before,
laying it neatly on the chair like an offering to the morning.
That morning, I slipped it on with a mix of excitement and
nerves. My white socks were pulled up straight, my hair
divided into two neat pigtails, each tied with a crisp white
bow. They gave life to the washed-out gray-blue color of my
shirtdress, tightened with a smocked apron just a little shorter
than the dress beneath it.

My notebooks were all covered in the same standard
blue paper — the kind meant to survive the entire school year,
though it rarely did. Inside my little brown *ghiozdan* (Romanian for satchel) were hand-me-down textbooks from the

previous first-graders, their pages softened by other small hands before mine.

And then, my treasure: a big wooden pencil box. Inside, three pencils, a few colored ones, and a shiny new eraser — the only thing truly mine, untouched by anyone else.

Mama had left a butter sandwich, a piece of apple pie, and one apple in the fridge — my lunch for the big day. "Put it in your *ghiozdan* just before you leave," she had instructed.

So I did, packing it carefully as if it were gold.

I glanced in the mirror before we left. My bows, my socks, the apron... I looked pretty. I wanted to give myself a little twirl, to watch the skirt float for me in approval.

But before I could finish, *Mamaia's* voice came from the hallway:

— "Let's go, Sophy. Stop that. You're good enough, I tell ya'."

We stepped out into the drizzle. *Mamaia* held her big black umbrella over both of us, but I carried my own — even though I didn't need it. Mama would have made sure I had one, and that alone made me want to use it.

It wasn't new — nothing really was — but it was mine now, passed down from Clara since kindergarten. Pale green-yellow, decorated with little black cats leaping around its canopy, it was my favorite thing in the world. The handle was shaped like a standing cat, its tiny body curving perfectly for my hand to grip.

But it was flimsy. Every time the wind blew, my precious umbrella flipped inside out, turning into a little water basin above my head. Each time, I twisted it back with stubborn determination, refusing to surrender.

People passing by smiled at the sight — a small girl clinging to a cat umbrella, battling the breeze like a tiny warrior.

The road to school was full of children. Most walked hand in hand with a parent, and some were lucky enough to have both. I watched those children bouncing between two loving hands, their laughter swinging like bungee cords of joy; and a wave of memories of Mama and Daddy together washed over me.

For a moment, my heart felt full — full of what once was, and of what I wished could be again.

Before I knew it, we were at the classroom door. My little umbrella was still dripping onto my shoes, my bows slightly damp. I took a deep breath.

Let's do this, I told myself — though deep inside, I wished I were still on that rainy road, holding Mama's hand in one and Daddy's in the other, walking toward a safety that felt endless.

I chose the first empty desk I saw — third desk in the third row, right by the window. A girl was already sitting there, but I barely had time to glance at her before a vigorous clatter rang out in the hallway.

A child came running past, shaking a heavy bell with all their might, loud and fast, announcing the start of class. I jumped in my seat. *What on earth was that?*
It was exactly 8 a.m.

And then he appeared — the teacher with the famous pointer.

"Good morning, children," he said with a serious smile that looked like it had been practiced in the mirror. "My name is *Tovarășul* Ior (comrade in Romanian), and I will be your teacher for the next four years. This year, and every year after, you will learn to read and write, you will learn numbers, and how to calculate…"

He lost me at read and write. My mind drifted instantly. Reading had always felt dull to me — just rows of lifeless letters with no pictures to dream about. I remembered trying to close Clara's book whenever she was absorbed in reading, wishing she would rather play with me. Or the sheets of her violin practice, full of strange twirling symbols that made no sense to my eyes. Books with no pictures had no magic for me.

"…and we will have sports activities, painting with watercolors, crafting…"

Now we're talking. I sat up straighter. I could do those things. I could do them better than anyone.

"I know how to craft and draw!" I blurted before I could stop myself.

The teacher stopped mid-sentence, looking over his glasses. "What is your name, little one?"

"I am Sophy," I said proudly.

"Sophy," he said, his voice turning stern, "whenever you wish to speak, you must raise your hand first. If I choose you, then you may talk. Until then, you stay quiet."

I didn't much care for his tone, but I quickly spotted a loophole: I could still talk if I raised my hand.

That first hour, my arm was in the air more than it was down.

And then, just like that, the bell rang again — loud and sharp, shaking the walls with freedom.

We had already "met" each other's names thanks to *Tovarășul* Ior's introductions, but I didn't remember a single one then. What I do remember is that somehow, everyone remembered mine.

"Sophy," they called, some curious, some already friendly. The classroom that had felt so big and cold began to soften. The gray walls didn't seem so heavy. The rows of wooden desks didn't look so strict. Something warm was starting to grow in the air — the first thread of familiarity.

The rest of the day was all about the *Abecedar* (Romanian ABC book)— the little book that promised to turn us into "proper readers and writers."

"This year," *Tovarășul* Ior said gravely, "you will learn the glamor of handwriting. We start with lines today… but by the end of the year, you will know it all."

We opened our ABC notebooks, their crisp pages smelling faintly of new paper and fear. He showed us the first three lines of the pattern we were to copy to the end of the page, then paced the rows, pointer stick tapping against his palm. Sometimes he'd stop and stare long at a child's page — the
silence thickening — before *Sfântu' Nicolae* (Saint Nicolas), as he called his multifunctional stick, came down to "correct"

the work.

I finished early — not perfect but done. He glanced at my page with a flicker of exasperation, as if expecting trouble. "You must do better," he said. "Next page — very good. Otherwise, you'll be the first to meet *Sfântu' Nicolae*."

I wasn't worried. I could do better.

So my eyes wandered — until my big wooden pencil box slid off the desk and hit the floor with a crack that made the whole room jump.

"I will have to talk to your mother," *Tovarășul* Ior announced, as if I had done it on purpose.

That afternoon, Mama got the call. He told her I'd been disruptive, asked too many questions — questions he said I'd "have to wait years to understand." He warned her that if it continued, he would "take measures."

Mama listened without protest. But when she hung up, she looked at me not with anger, but with the kind of kindness that makes you want to do better.

And I did want to. I just wasn't sure if I could.

School went on like that for a while — between my meetings with *Sfântu' Nicolae* and the constant comparisons to Clara, the "ideal" student.

During sports class, while others followed the rules, I turned the schoolyard into my gymnastics stage, cartwheeling to the awe of my classmates. Even *Tovarășul* Ior clapped once or twice — though I don't think he meant to.

And then there was my favorite game: making him talk about anything but the lesson.

"E… from Elephant," he wrote one morning.

My hand shot up. "Elephants… what country do they live in?"

"Africa," he said.

"But I saw on *Teleenciclopedia* (a Saturday TV Info Program) there are elephants in Asia too!"

"Yes," he said slowly, "but they look different."

"Then why did you say Africa? Are there more there? We have some at the Zoo. Could Romania have elephants one day?"

One question led to another, until the whole class was asking about lions, giraffes, and crocodiles — and the lesson on the letter E was long gone.

I might not have been the quiet, sweet student Clara was.

But I was the one who made school… interesting.

~ ~ ~ ~ ~ ✦ ~ ~ ~ ~ ~

What Life Whispered to Me

There are no straight lines in the soul's journey.
Only paths that twist and rise,
shaped by questions too wild for rules
and dreams too vast for order.

As children, we are not born to walk in lines drawn
by others.
We are born to wander,
to wonder,
to spill over the edges of what the world thinks is
"enough."

Authority calls it mischief.
Society calls it disobedience.
But life itself knows better:
curiosity is the first language of truth,
and freedom begins in the hearts of little ones who
dare to ask,
"Why must the world be only this way?"

To nurture a child is not to tame them.
It is to stand guard over their fire
and let their questions burn holes
through the cages we have mistaken for wisdom.

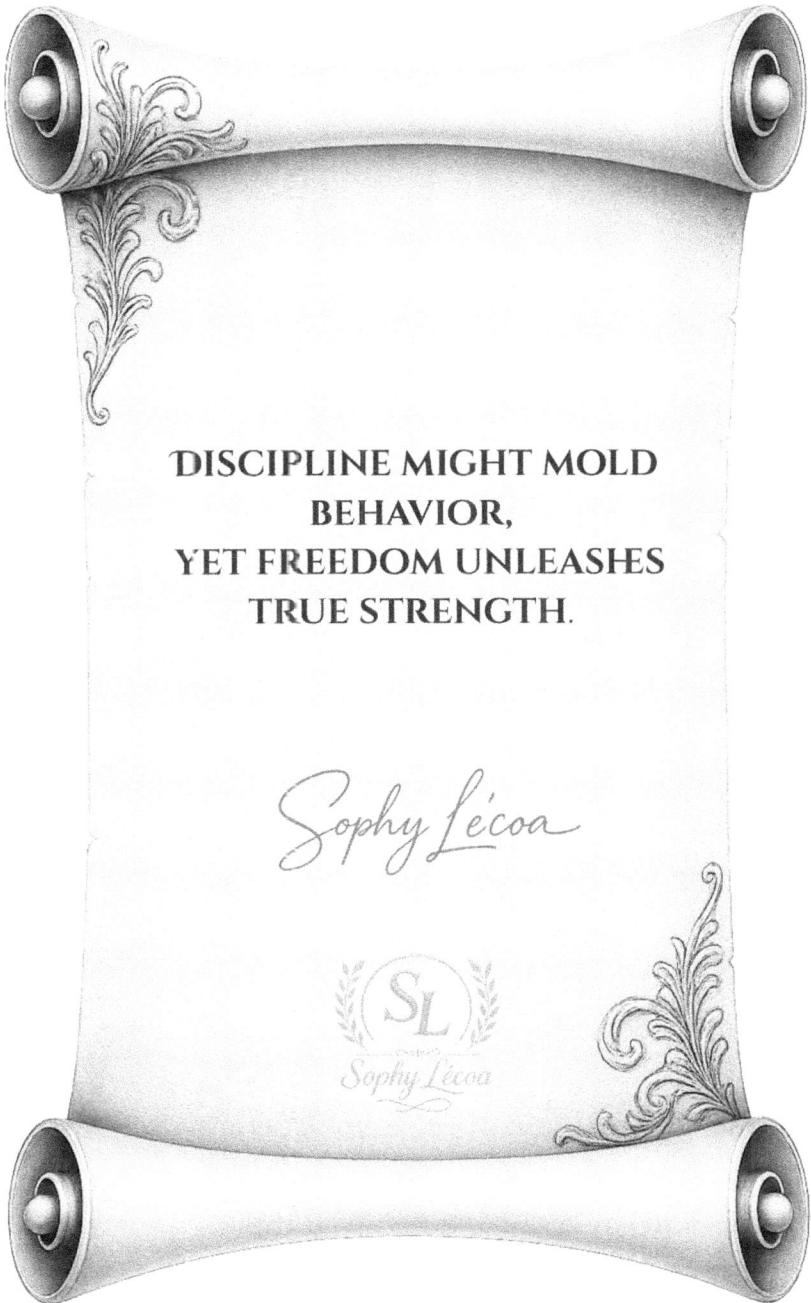

DISCIPLINE MIGHT MOLD
BEHAVIOR,
YET FREEDOM UNLEASHES
TRUE STRENGTH.

Sophy Lécoa

Chapter 8

The Book That Changed Everything

My only real trouble in school wasn't asking too many
questions,
or meeting *Sfântu' Nicolae* too often —
it was reading.
I hated it.
Every time it was my turn to read a passage out loud,
my stomach twisted into hard little knots.
My throat tightened,
my eyes darted over the lines like they were foreign
 language,
and I could feel my cheeks burn hot with embarrassment
while my classmates' eyes followed me.
The words tangled in my mouth,
came out in jerks and stops,

and the sound of my own stuttering felt like it echoed in that
silent classroom.

     Homework reading?
I never practiced.
By then,
I was still tugging on Clara's sleeve on Saturday nights,
whispering for translations during the rare foreign films
that flickered onto our black-and-white TV.
The static hissed faintly in the quiet room
while the soft glow of the screen lit our faces.
"No, Sophy!" she'd scold, exasperated.
"For the love of God, learn to read!"

     It didn't feel good to hear…
but my stubbornness was bigger than my shame.

     Tovarășul Ior didn't let it go, either.
His endless phone calls home became the soundtrack to my
afternoons —
his voice sharp and clipped even from a distance:
"She needs to read more, Comrade Le'coa.
Small print from the newspapers every night —
that's the only solution."

     The newspapers! I thought, horrified.
Those dreary, gray pages smelling faintly of ink,
covered with black-and-white pictures of our *"dear leader"* …
It was the worst punishment I could imagine.

     One evening,
I was sitting cross-legged on my bed,
needle in hand,
whispering to Luiza, my long-suffering doll,

promising her that this time,
the pink thread I was sewing into her bald scalp
would make her truly beautiful.

  The door creaked open.
My heart jumped
and I snatched her under the blanket in a single movement,
my hand flying to rest on the *Abecedar* book, pretending I'd
just set it down in case *Mamaia* was the one coming in.

  But it wasn't *Mamaia.*
It was Mama.

  My heart leapt in a different way —
a warm, rushing joy.
She stepped quietly into the room,
her coat still smelling faintly of the outside —
damp air, worn leather,
and a trace of her perfume.
She sat down beside me,
her eyes soft,
her hands still chilled from the evening air.

  Without a word,
she reached into her bag.
My pulse quickened —
I was already picturing Chinese chocolate…
or maybe, just maybe,
a stick of cinnamon chewing gum.

  But no.
She pulled out a book.

  My excitement fell with a thud.
"That's a thick book…" I said,

suspicion dripping from my voice,
no trace of enthusiasm.

Mama just smiled —
the kind of smile that didn't need defending.
"This is for me, not for you," she said.
"I found something in here I want to read to you."

My heart softened instantly.
Mama, reading me a story?
That was magic.

I plumped my pillow,
tugged the blanket higher,
and waited.

"The book is called *Coliba Unchiului Tom* (+Uncle Tom's
Cabin+)," she began.
And then she read.

And suddenly,
I wasn't in our small apartment anymore.
I was inside that story.
The room around me faded
until all that existed was her voice —
low, warm, steady —
and the images her words painted in my mind.

My chest tightened and released with each turn of the
tale,
my heart racing
as if I was living every moment on those pages.
I didn't even notice
how tightly I was clutching Luiza
until Mama's voice fell silent.

She closed the book gently,
as if it were something sacred.
"Isn't it a great story?" she asked,
a knowing sparkle lighting her tired eyes.

"Mama, read more, please!" I begged,
my hands clasped together like I was praying.
I meant it with all of me.

Mama shook her head,
smiling as if she had just given me a secret.
She set the book beside me.
"If you want to know more," she said softly,
"here it is.
You can find out yourself."

She kissed my forehead,
the press of her lips lingering like a blessing,
and left the room.

I stared at that book for a long moment.
Then something inside me shifted.
I jumped, grabbed it,
and began to read —
haltingly at first,
my lips moving,
my finger following each word like a guide.
Then faster.
Smoother.

The more I read,
the more the words seemed to open like windows.
I read and read,

long after the lights should have been out,
my eyes straining in the dim glow.

By the time I turned the last page of *Uncle Tom's Cabin*
two weeks later,
something inside me had changed forever.

My confidence soared.
At school,
I raised my hand for my turn to read —
no fear,
no stuttering,
no more shame.

And I never stopped reading books again.

~ ~ ~ ~ ~ ✧ ~ ~ ~ ~ ~

What Life Whispered to Me

We don't know what we don't know.
Until a gentle hand places it before us —
and something ancient stirs within.

Mama didn't tell me what to see in those pages.
She simply opened the doorway
and let me find the light myself.

That is the quiet genius of a mother's wisdom —
not to fill us with her answers,
but to awaken the knowing
that has been sleeping in us all along.

— Sophy Le'coa

~ ~ ~ ~ ~ ✦ ~ ~ ~ ~ ~

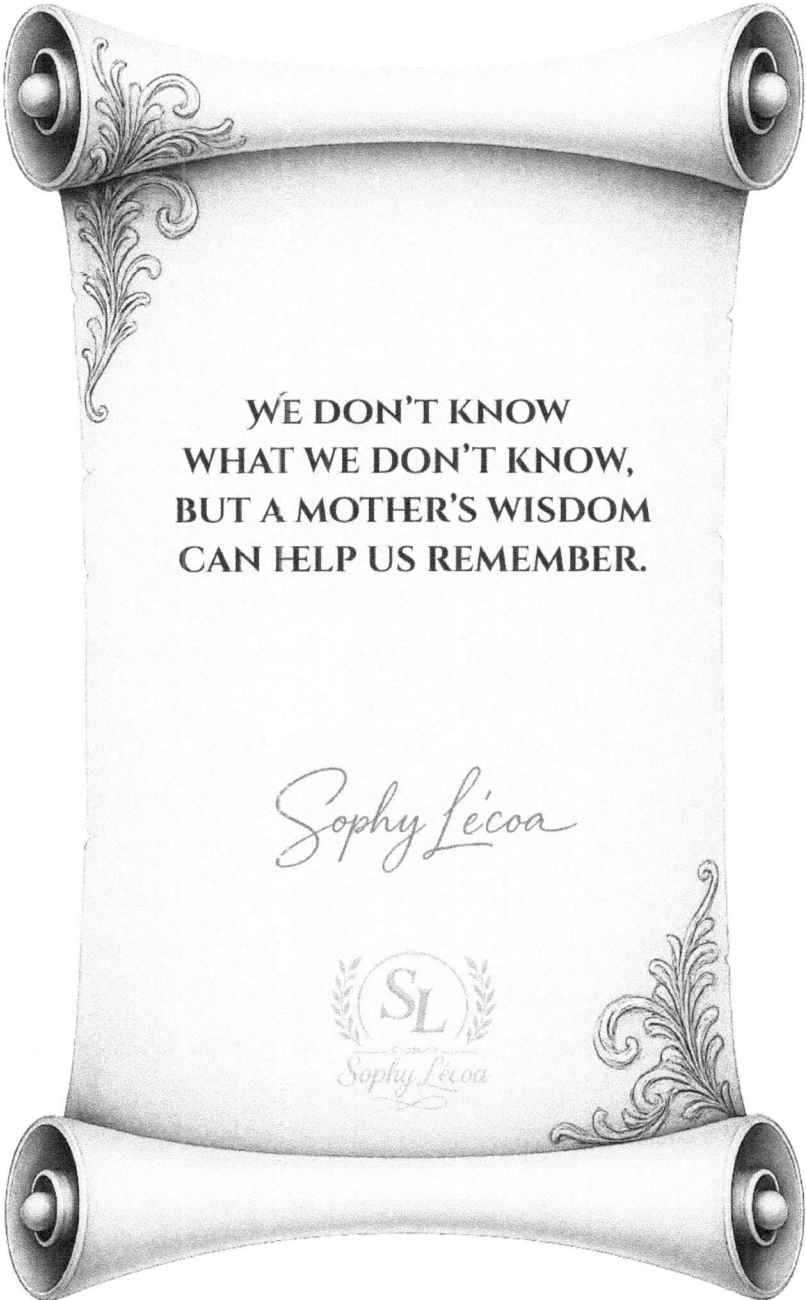

WE DON'T KNOW
WHAT WE DON'T KNOW,
BUT A MOTHER'S WISDOM
CAN HELP US REMEMBER.

Sophy Lécoa

Chapter 9

Graduation Day

The end-of-school celebration finally arrived — a day so important in Communist Romania that even the sky seemed to hold its breath.

The air was already warm, the kind that clung to your skin, and in the courtyard every student from first to eighth grade stood in perfect squared *careu* formation. Shoes shuffled softly on the sunbaked pavement. The smell of dust and freshly cut flowers — gathered for the ceremony — mingled in the air like two strangers forced to dance.

Clara, far away in the fifth-grade section, glanced at me across the crowd. Just a small, knowing smile. But that was enough. My heart steadied. I felt safer just knowing she was somewhere out there.

Mama stood with the other parents at the back, her face drawn from endless hospital shifts, but her eyes scanning the rows like a lighthouse beam through fog. My heart pounded

— not because of the songs, or the flowers, or the promise of a diploma, but because she was here.

The ceremony began as they all did: patriotic songs, poems praising our "dear leaders," *Nicolae and Elena Ceaușescu*, for the "*rich and prosperous country*" they had "*given*" us — "everything we needed and more." Even as a child, I knew how hollow it was, but we sang because that's what you did.

The teachers stood on the school steps like soldiers on parade, delivering speeches about the year's "great achievements." Their words drifted into the heat like dust — too heavy to rise — yet they puffed with pride as if they had built us into something extraordinary.

Our uniforms were as stiff as the speeches. We first graders wore *Șoimii Patriei*: bright orange nylon shirts, blue skirts or shorts, stubby blue ties fastened tight at the neck. The older students were *Pionieri*, in white shirts, red scarves, and black pants or pleated skirts. Every girl had the same elastic white headband, every boy the same clipped haircut. Uniformity was the point — in communism, no one was meant to stand out.

But inside me, my little heart was a *firecracker*.

Every child clutched a bouquet for their teacher. Mine was big — almost too big for my hands — but I held it tight, waiting for my name. I imagined Mama's face when she saw me walk up, her pride wrapping me like sunlight.

At last, after an eternity of other names and polite applause, mine was called. I stepped forward, feet steady on the warm pavement. The teacher handed me my diploma and prize, saying the same solemn words he'd said to everyone else. I barely heard them; I forgot to hand him the flowers too —I was already halfway in my mind to Mama.

When the ceremony ended, the lines dissolved, the leaders' names faded, and I ran — bouquet in one hand, diploma in the other — straight into her arms.

"Mama, look!" I said breathlessly, holding up my prize like treasure.

She knelt, pulling me close, her eyes shining.
"Oh, Sophy… I'm proud of you. So proud of both my girls."

Clara appeared, waving her own diploma, and Mama hugged us both, kissing the tops of our heads like we were her whole world — and we were.

Then she said the words that turned the day into a true celebration:
"Let's go to *cofetărie*." (sweets shop)

We walked hand in hand through the gray streets, toward the little sweet shop that always felt like another world. Outside was cracked concrete and peeling paint; inside, the air smelled of sugar and small dreams. Six cakes sat under glass — the same ones we always saw, lined up like obedient soldiers.

Clara and I rushed to the counter, pointing as if we didn't already know what we'd choose. Mama laughed, ordered three slices, and we sat near the window, the afternoon light spilling across our table.

The cakes were greasy, heavy, and unchanging — except for the frosting color — but that day, they tasted like victory. My feet swung under the chair as I took a bite, thinking about Mama in the schoolyard, about Clara's grin when she ran to me.

And in that small corner of our gray world, the sweetness was ours to share.

Not the speeches.

Not the uniforms.

Not the "dear leader."

Just Mama, Clara, and me — three girls celebrating a small, hard-won triumph, making it feel like everything we could ever need.

Then Mama leaned back and said, almost casually, "Girls, I have something important to tell you later, when we get home…"

When we opened the apartment door, we were met — bam! — with the heavy perfume of *Mamaia's* legendary soap battling the sharp tang of cabbage soup, each smell fighting for dominance in our tiny kitchen.

"Hello, *Mamaia*!" I called, my voice breaking into a half-gag, half-greeting.

Clara burst out laughing as we darted to the living room.

"Sophy, your gag just made me wanna gag too!"

"Clara, this is serious!" I gasped, clutching my stomach. "One more whiff and you'll see my cake in reverse!"

"Just breathe through your mouth," she advised between giggles.

"But I can smell it through my ears, Clara!" I wailed.

That broke her. She laughed so hard the couch shook, and like always, I followed until my belly hurt, the smell forgotten.

When we finally calmed, sprawled on the couch, my mind wandered to Mama's "big announcement."

"Clara," I whispered, "do you think Mama's going to tell us the stork is bringing us a baby brother or sister?"

She gave me a look like I'd just asked if the moon could bake a pie.
"Nooo, silly. You need a daddy to have a baby."

"Why does the stork need a daddy?"

She hesitated, sighed like a fifth-grader who'd seen the world.
"I don't really know. But it's a must."

"Hmm… maybe we'll get another daddy then."

Clara stared at the ceiling, then said softly, "I don't think so, Sophy."

"What about Mr. E?" I asked. "He fixes the sink sometimes… *like Daddy used to.*"

Her eyes widened — then she giggled, swatting my arm. "Nooo! He's just the plumber."

I grinned, half-believing my own idea. "Maybe Mama will surprise us one day. She'll walk in and say, *'Tadaaa!'* — and there he is, a brand-new daddy."

Clara shook her head, still laughing. And for a moment, before the grown-up truths came, we stayed in that little bubble — two sisters, dreaming silly dreams, safe in the sound of our own laughter.

What Life Whispered to Me

Our childhood held a secret kind of alchemy —
the power to turn the steam of soap and cabbage into
laughter,
games, and shared dreams between two sisters.

Back then, we didn't know to call it a miracle.
We simply lived inside it.

Only later, when we began to understand the weight
our grown-ups carried,
did we realize how fragile that magic had been —
and how rare the courage of love that blossoms in
scarcity
without ever asking for anything in return.

Life whispered to me then, and still does today:
true wealth is not what we hold in our hands,
but the power to love and to laugh
even when the world feels like it has left no space for
either. — *Sophy Le'coa*

~ ~ ~ ~ ~ ✧ ~ ~ ~ ~ ~ ~

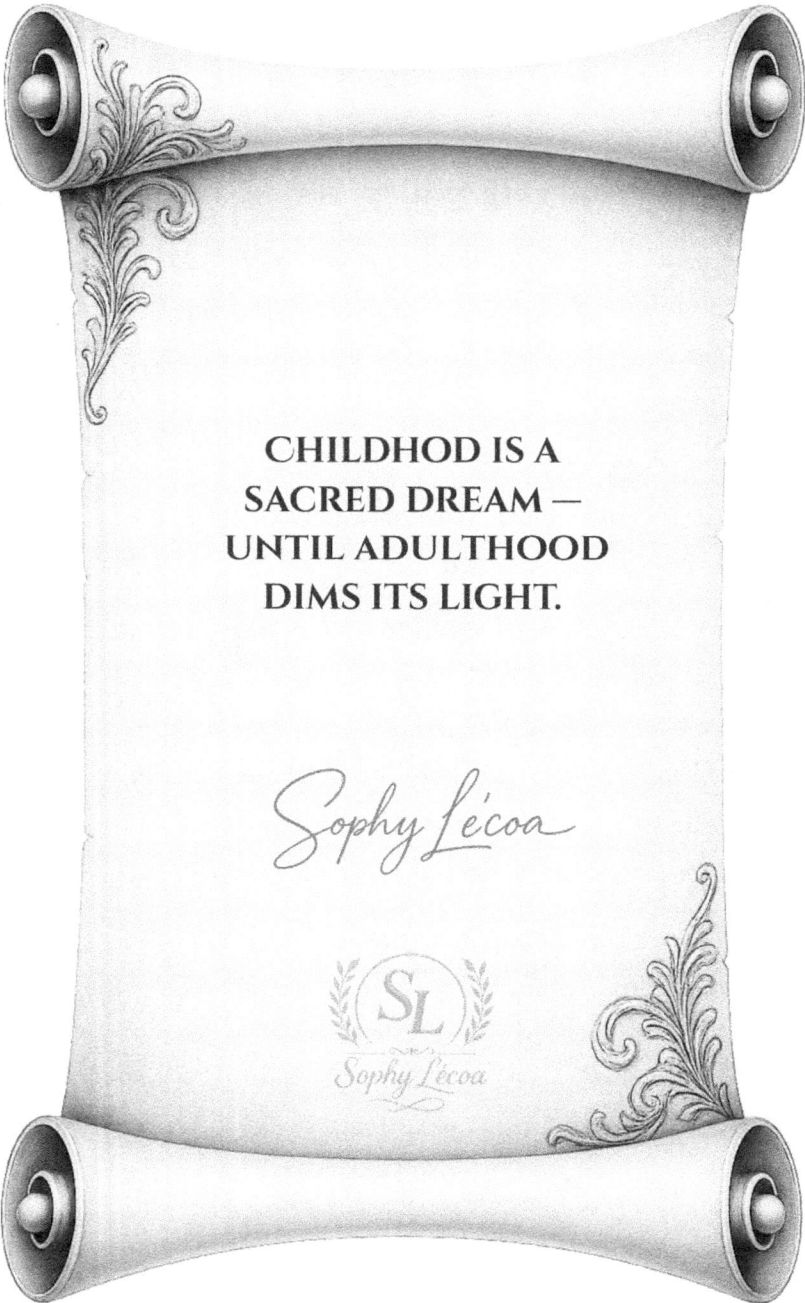

CHILDHOD IS A
SACRED DREAM —
UNTIL ADULTHOOD
DIMS ITS LIGHT.

Sophy Lécoa

Chapter 10

Mama's Truth

Mama came to us, still wearing that soft smile that had the power to lift the weight off any day. But her eyes... they shifted now, turning serious — not angry, not playful, but carrying that sacred tone we recognized instantly. It was the tone that meant every word to follow would matter.

Before she could speak, my question burst out, unpolished and unplanned:
"Mama... are we going to have a new daddy?"

Her face softened, surprised by the leap my little mind had made. But her voice stayed calm, anchored.
"What? No, love. Why would you ask something like that?"

I hesitated, fidgeting with my fingers, my courage shrinking. "I just thought... *maybe*..."

She took a slow breath and crouched down, so her face was level with ours. Her voice was gentle, but there was steel woven through the softness.

"Listen to me, both of you. I will never, ever replace your daddy with anyone. Not as long as I live."

"But why, Mama?" I whispered, needing a reason my heart could hold.

Her gaze moved from me to Clara, as though sealing a vow with both of us.

"Because I don't want any other man close to my little girls."

There was a fierceness beneath her words that felt like a shield settling around us — invisible, but unbreakable. *I didn't fully understand it then, but I felt its power.*

She straightened, her serious eyes softening just enough to draw us in. Taking both our hands in hers, warm and steady, she spoke our full names — Sophia, Clarita — *the way she only did when something truly mattered.*

"As I said, I have something important to share with you."

We were already on the couch, our small legs dangling over the edge. Mama crossed the room to the armoire, opened its creaky door, and pulled out her old brown leather clutch — the one that seemed to carry more than money. It carried her quiet battles, her daily courage, her untold sacrifices.

She sat between us, the clutch letting out a tired sigh as she opened it.

One by one, she began to place small bundles of bills in our hands.

First, into Clara's:

"This is for our home. The mortgage."

Another bundle:

"This is for the light, the heat, the phone."

74

Another:

"This is for food — only what we need."

Then the smallest bundle of all:

"Clara, this is for when your clothes don't fit anymore."

I waited, holding my breath, certain that my turn would be different. Mama reached in again, pulled out a small folded scrap of recycled paper — no bills beneath it — and placed it in my palm, closing my fingers gently over it. "This is the extra, Sophy," she said quietly. "But for now… there's nothing here."

The paper was weightless, but the truth it carried was heavy. I searched her eyes, looking for embarrassment, shame, defeat. But there was none. Only honesty — and the fatigue of someone who works for every breath in the day.

Clasping her hands together, she looked at both of us. "This is what I have every month. I will not borrow. I will not beg. I will not ask for what I cannot give. So please… don't come to me asking for sweets at the market, or toys in the window. Not because I don't love you — but because I will not lie to you."

Something shifted inside me then.

I didn't feel poor.

I felt… trusted.

Mama had just made us partners in something bigger than money — a promise to live with dignity and without shame, no matter how little we had.

Clara nodded, solemn as though she were twenty instead of ten.

I clutched that empty slip of paper like it was treasure — not for the money it lacked, but for the truth it held, and for the fact that Mama had trusted me to keep it.

In that moment, I understood that love could look like sacrifice,
and sacrifice could feel like strength.
The slip of paper might have been empty,
but it carried a wealth no coin could measure —
a wealth that would shape the way I saw trust, dignity, and love
for the rest of my life.

~ ~ ~ ~ ~ ✧ ~ ~ ~ ~ ~

What Life Whispered to Me

Not all poverty is the same.
There is the kind born of laziness —
a poverty that chooses idleness and then complains of
hunger.
And then there is the kind forced upon you by a sys-
tem
that takes your strength, your hours, your youth…
and gives you almost nothing in return.
The first is a wound you give yourself.
The second is a theft committed against your very
breath.
Mama's hands carried the marks of the second kind
—
the poverty of those who work until their bones ache,
yet live as if in a labor camp without walls.
And still, she gave us more than money could buy:
trust instead of deceit,
dignity instead of shame.
That was her rebellion,

her quiet victory in a world that tried to make her
bow.

And in that victory, she taught us what true wealth
was.
A wealth that cannot be measured in coins,
but in the courage to stand unbroken.
A wealth that belongs to anyone who chooses dignity
over despair.

"True wealth is not counted in coins, but in the courage to stand unbroken."

— Sophy Le'coa

~ ~ ~ ~ ~ ✧ ~ ~ ~ ~ ~

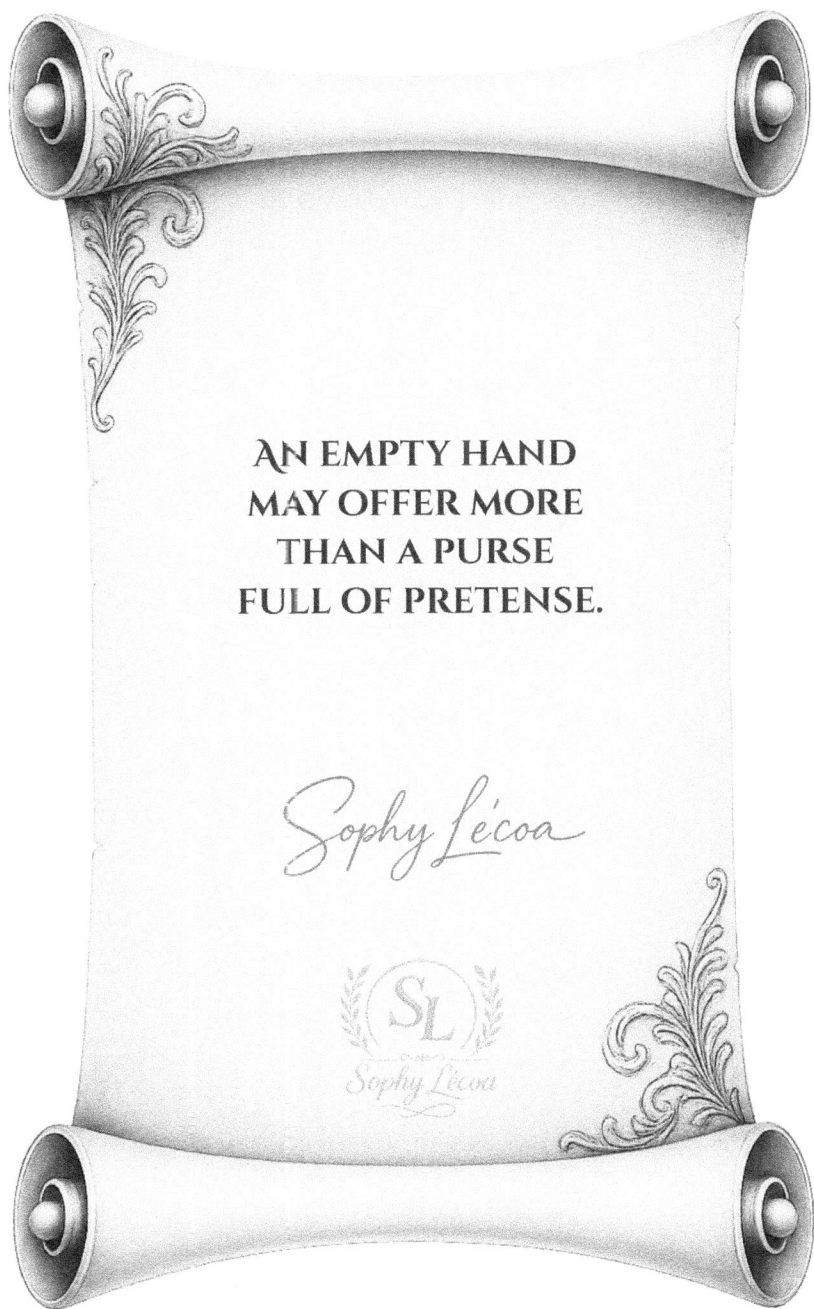

AN EMPTY HAND
MAY OFFER MORE
THAN A PURSE
FULL OF PRETENSE.

Sophy Lécoa

Chapter 11

Missing Teeth and Law Practice

That summer, I lost my two front teeth.
But what I gained was far more valuable:
the art of persuasion — a skill sharp enough to make even the
sternest adults fold like laundry on a Sunday afternoon.

Mama finally agreed to let Clara and me spend time in
the countryside with her older brother's family. To us, it felt
like freedom — no *Mamaia* watching over every crumb we
dropped or every giggle that got too loud. But that freedom
came with a catch: we missed Mama every single day.

Life in the village moved to a different rhythm. Our
cousin Mia, just two years older than me, already worked like
a grown-up. From sunrise to sunset, she was a blur of motion
— feeding chickens, chasing stray goats, hauling buckets of
water from the well, planting rows of beans, and gathering
vegetables until her arms were full and her braid damp with

sweat. By the time the Cooperativa truck rumbled in to collect their share, the family's baskets were nearly emptied of their best.

Somehow, though, there was always plenty of *slăninuță* (thick, smoky bacon), served with green onions and slices of fresh, still-warm bread. The taste was so good I kept smacking my lips, my eyes rolling with pleasure, which made Uncle Eri smile. It felt like a feast fit for queens.

Even breakfast had its own... twist.
Every morning, the adults handed us kids a tiny shot glass of *pălincă* (Romania's fiery plum brandy) — "for appetite and good digestion." It burned down my throat like liquid fire, but they weren't wrong — after that, I could have eaten the table if they'd let me. Even Clara, usually a shy little bird at meals, devoured everything in sight. And yet, both of us stayed skinny as twigs.

Days were long, but not for us. There was no running water, only the deep stone well and a big metal basin for washing. The outhouse stood far from the house, leaning slightly as if it wanted to escape its own smell. At night, I'd lie awake, wide-eyed, counting the minutes until daylight so I could avoid that dark path.

Evenings made everything worth it. Neighbors gathered at someone's front gate, swapping stories, passing around steaming potatoes from a cauldron meant for the pigs. We each got one, sprinkled with coarse salt, and sat on the ground listening to tales that sometimes had us rolling in the dust laughing, and other times clutching each other's arms, swearing we'd never go near the cemetery again.

And oh, the freedom! We tore through meadows dotted with red poppies, chased butterflies until our legs ached, tumbled into haystacks and splashed barefoot in the river. Dirt on our faces, mud on our clothes, twigs in our hair — nobody cared. It was heaven.

Except for one thing: Mia couldn't always join us. She was too busy working, and Clara hated it.

"Go on, Sophy," she whispered one day, eyes gleaming with mischief. "You're the only one who can make Uncle Eri say yes."

I puffed up my chest. She was right. I was almost seven — practically a professional negotiator.

I skipped over to Uncle Eri, my arms swinging loose and innocent, my gap-toothed smile wide. My head tilted just so, like a child from a postcard — pure sugar wrapped in pigtails.

"Uncle Eri," I began softly, "you know how much I love coming here, right?"

He leaned on his pitchfork, one eyebrow raised. "Of course, Sophy."

I clasped my hands behind my back, rocking on my toes like I was asking for nothing bigger than an extra cookie. "Do you know how far the city is?" I asked, drawing it out as if the answer might change our fate.

"Yeah, it's far," he said, half-smiling already.

I widened my eyes, adding a tiny sigh. "And do you know how hard it is for me to get here?"

He chuckled. "Your mama brings you."

"Yes, but…" My voice softened, then sharpened with urgency. My little hands flew into the air. "Do you know what it takes to get her to bring us? We beg, Uncle Eri. All. Year. Long."

By now, every "t" and "s" whistled through my missing teeth, spraying the summer air just enough to make him blink. Clara was already hiding behind the water bucket, shoulders shaking with silent laughter.

"And now," I said, planting my hands on my hips like a miniature lawyer, "we're finally here… and Mia can't even play with us?"

Then came my closing argument — the one no jury could resist. I tilted my head, blinked slowly, leaned in just a little too close, and whispered with all the gravity my seven years could muster:

"Don't you love me, Uncle Eri?"

Silence. The kind that falls when a grown man realizes he's been cornered by a gap-toothed child with an airtight case. He wiped his face — maybe from the heat, maybe from the effort of not laughing — and sighed.

"Fine, Sophy," he said, shaking his head but smiling. "Mia can play. But if trouble comes…"

"Yayy!" I squealed, throwing my arms into the air like a champion. Clara burst into laughter, and Mia dashed over to join us, free at last.

It felt like we had won the summer.

It started with the haystack — a towering, perfect stack built for the winter feed. Hours of sweaty work had gone into it. It took us less than two hours to destroy it. We climbed, rolled, jumped, and somersaulted until it looked like a storm had torn through. We were laughing so hard we couldn't breathe.

Right until the shouting started.

We got sent home early after that.

And there, like a hawk on a branch, was *Mamaia*. Word traveled fast in the countryside.

Her "lesson" in proper behavior began instantly. She shoved us into the tub with just enough lukewarm water to cover the bottom — which cooled faster than we could blink — and scrubbed us raw as if we were two filthy rugs. Then she discovered the small army of lice we'd brought home. Out came the lamp oil and the fine-tooth comb, dragging through our hair with the force of a soldier polishing his boots. Our scalps burned, our eyes watered, and still we giggled under our breath at the memory of flying through that hay like wild birds.

That summer, I learned three things:

Hard work feeds people but leaves little room for wonder.

Trouble tastes sweeter with good company.

And with a fearless grin, relentless charm, and spat every word like a dare, even grown-ups' rules can bend —

at least for a while.

~ ~ ~ ~ ~ ✧ ~ ~ ~ ~ ~

What Life Whispered to Me

*True power doesn't always sit in big offices or wear
serious faces.*
*Sometimes, it's a gap-toothed kid with a smile sharp
enough to slice through the sternest rules,*
a fearless grin that hides its own history of battles,
*and a heart stubborn enough to ask for more joy than
the world is willing to give.*

*My smile was my weapon — not to hurt, but to sof-
ten,*
*to make people believe in the possibility of yes when
no felt set in stone.*

And maybe that's how change begins —
with someone small, relentless, and smiling,
refusing to accept no as the final word.

— Sophy Le'coa

~ ~ ~ ~ ~ ✧ ~ ~ ~ ~ ~

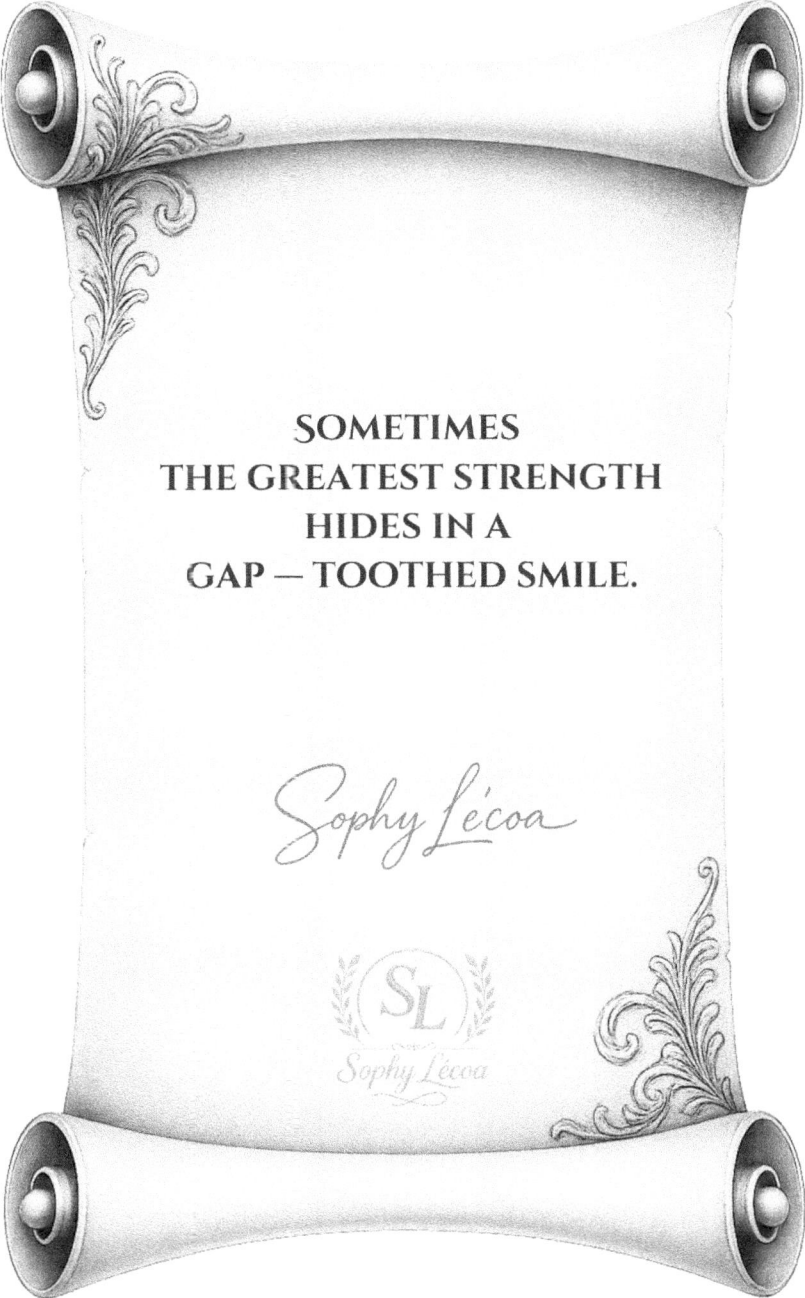

SOMETIMES
THE GREATEST STRENGTH
HIDES IN A
GAP — TOOTHED SMILE.

Sophy Lécoa

Chapter 12

The Thick Pajama

The Coldest Nights

I remember that winter vividly, because it was the one when the nights began to swallow the light — and with it, the warmth. Power cuts became as predictable as the sunset, and once the electricity died, so did the heat. The kerosene lamp and candles moved permanently into our lives like unwanted guests, casting thin shadows on walls that seemed to grow colder by the hour.

The blackouts had a reason: the government called it *"saving for prosperity."* We called it surviving.

That day, it was so cold I felt like every breath would freeze my brain. Snow piled high outside, and I still had gymnastics practice — twenty-five minutes away by bus. I was a big girl now, at eight years old, going there and back all on my own.

The buses were always crowded — packed like sardines in a can — but lately, it had gotten so bad the doors couldn't even close, people spilling out and clinging to each other like grapes refusing to fit into a basket. And when your stop was coming up, you had to fight with everything you had to reach the door and break free. That was the city now: pure torture on wheels.

When practice ended, so did the power. The buses stopped dead, their two metal legs disconnected from the spiderweb of wires above. It took me almost three hours to get home, cutting through every back road and shortcut I knew. By the time I arrived, my face was red as a tomato. Mama was already gone to her second shift, but *Mamaia* was there. She hugged me — not like Mama, but still a hug — and pulled me toward the stove where all four burners glowed faintly, giving off what little heat they could.

That night was so cold that all the blankets we had weren't enough. Clara and I layered sweaters, gloves, hats, even our winter coats. Once we were all bundled, I turned to her:

"Clara — make me laugh. I get warm when I laugh."

"Mmm, let me think," she murmured from under the blanket up to her nose.

"I can't think right now, Sophy."

"Me neither," I said. "I think this cold will make us dumb."

That did it. She laughed first, then me, but even our laughter felt frozen in our throats.

By morning, frost had kissed our noses red. We jumped around the room, teasing each other about whose was worse, until we were warm enough to shuffle into the tiny kitchen. There we huddled with Mama and *Mamaia*, hands stretched over one lonely eye of the stove.

Even as we laughed at our frozen noses, something shifted in me. I realized the cold wasn't just in our house. It was everywhere, in everyone's life. That was the beginning of how winters were spent under communism.

And we learned early: never talk about it. In Romania back then, even the frost had ears.

The Lines and the Butter Plan

Looking back, I think that was when life started to feel truly bad for everyone. Maybe it had always been that way, but now Clara and I were old enough to notice — old enough to be pulled into it.

Lines. Endless, merciless lines. For hours, for anything, if luck was on your side.

I began to understand there were two kinds of poverty. The kind born of laziness — when people don't work but still complain of hunger. And then the kind you're forced into, even when you work harder than ever, even when you give every drop of yourself to labor that doesn't pay and still go home to bare shelves and ration cards. That was our kind.

Gas lines were the worst — stretching for kilometers even though most people barely owned cars.

Even Driving was rationed to *every other Sunday*, yet the lines snaked on as if hope itself had queued up and fallen asleep.

But it wasn't just gas. All over the city, lines coiled like pythons around entire blocks, heavy and unyielding. Sometimes they inched forward. Sometimes they didn't move at all. And strangest of all often, we didn't even know what we were waiting for.

You'd tug at someone's sleeve.
"What are they selling?"
"I don't know. But everyone's waiting, so..."

And that was enough. Hope was contagious.

Word of mouth spread faster than fire: a shipment was coming — maybe oil, maybe cocoa, maybe shoes. By the time you heard, the line had already formed. And once you caught one, you stayed. For hours. In biting cold or scorching heat. Hoping. Always hoping.

And sometimes, after all that, you'd reach the door only to hear the flat words drop like a stone in your stomach:
"It's finished."

That was it. You didn't argue. You just walked away, empty-handed, because the line had already stolen every ounce of your strength. Maybe tomorrow would be different.

Chickens? Rare — like winning the lottery.
Salami? A brief appearance.
Bologna? If luck was kind.
Lemons? A miracle.
And soap? Always *Cheia*. Big gray blocks that smelled like despair — but still better than *Mamaia's* scratchy, homemade bars.

Once a month, we had ration cards — *cartele*. Square paper listing our family name, the number of mouths, and rows for bread, flour, sugar, eggs, oil. Each purchase was marked with a hole punched like a scar. By year's end, the more holes you had, small victories you had survived.

And then there was grocery bag status. We all carried a sad-looking *plasa de rafie* (raffia bag), big and strong enough to carry a small caw. But, if you carried a plastic bag with "Walmart," "Marlboro," or any Western logo, you weren't carrying groceries — you were carrying prestige. Proof the outside world existed. Those bags weren't folded. They were reused until they turned to lace.

Inside the store, echoes bounced off empty shelves. The butcher's hooks hung bare, waiting. The freezers held only fish — pale, frozen stiff, stacked in perfect rows, their glassy eyes staring through the ice. Sometimes Mama would pause there, wondering if she should try again. But the last time, when she defrosted it, it disintegrated into nothing.

Every morning, we were guaranteed one thing: dairy. Milk, butter, sour cream, yogurt. But only one per person. If you were late, you might get nothing.

So, Clara and I devised a plan — to beat the system.

We'd get to the store before sunrise, line up at the front. When the crowd formed, we'd split. One at the front, one farther back. When the store opened, I'd sneak up to Clara, my bag holding my spot behind. Two portions of butter at the front. Then Clara would "visit" me later — and we'd get two more.

Four butters. Two girls. One foolproof plan.

Except… when we arrived, the line was already long. Some people had slept outside. Worse — everyone was trying the same trick. Sneaking forward, doubling back, reappearing like ghosts of socialism.

I looked at Clara, wide-eyed.

"How is it possible… that everyone had the same idea?"

And then it hit me.

"It's the fish," I whispered. "They must be putting something in it."

We cracked up quietly. And honestly — a part of me still thinks I was right.

The Day I Broke a Little

This insanity went on six days a week. Sunday was our only pause — one breath before diving back in.

One Saturday during gymnastics practice, a teammate whispered that her grandpa had rushed to the store, the one in our neighborhood. They had just brought in bananas.

My chest nearly burst with joy.

Bananas!

I knew Mama would get one for us. The rest of practice, I flew — tumbling and leaping as if the air itself was sweet with the *promise of that golden fruit.*

I rushed home, barely breathing. Mama was in the kitchen.

"Mama, did you get at least one banana?"

She turned, puzzled. "Sophy, what are you talking about?"

"*Bananas*, Mama — *bananas*! They sold them today at the store down the street. Silvia's grandpa told her!"

"I didn't know, baby. I'm so sorry."

"Oh, Mama…" And then the tears came. Hot, unstoppable. I crumpled to the floor, crying harder than I ever had.

She gathered me in her arms, rocking me. "Oh, Sophy, it's okay, little baby… please don't cry."

But I had to. And in a strange way, *it felt good to finally let it out.*

Without a word, Mama grabbed three bars of soap and two packs of cigarettes and hurried out. Later I learned she had gone straight to Silvia's house, hoping to trade for just one banana. But they hadn't been lucky either. The fruit was gone before they knew it.

~ ~ ~ ~ ~ ✧ ~ ~ ~ ~ ~

What Life Whispered to Me

The bus swayed and groaned, a moving cage of winter breath and tired faces. Shoulders pressed against me, coats scratched my face, the stale air of a city holding its breath weighed heavy.

It would be easier to stay. To wait.
To tell myself I'd try next time.

But I had learned something in those crowded

winters: the true prison is not the metal walls that hold you.
It's the quiet agreement you make with fear to stay where you are.

So, I pushed forward. A step. An elbow.
A breath of cold air leaking through the cracks of the door.

And when it finally opened, I spilled into the street like a bird breaking free from its cage. The night air bit my cheeks, but I was smiling — because I knew the bus hadn't decided where I would end up.

I had. *— Sophy Le'coa*

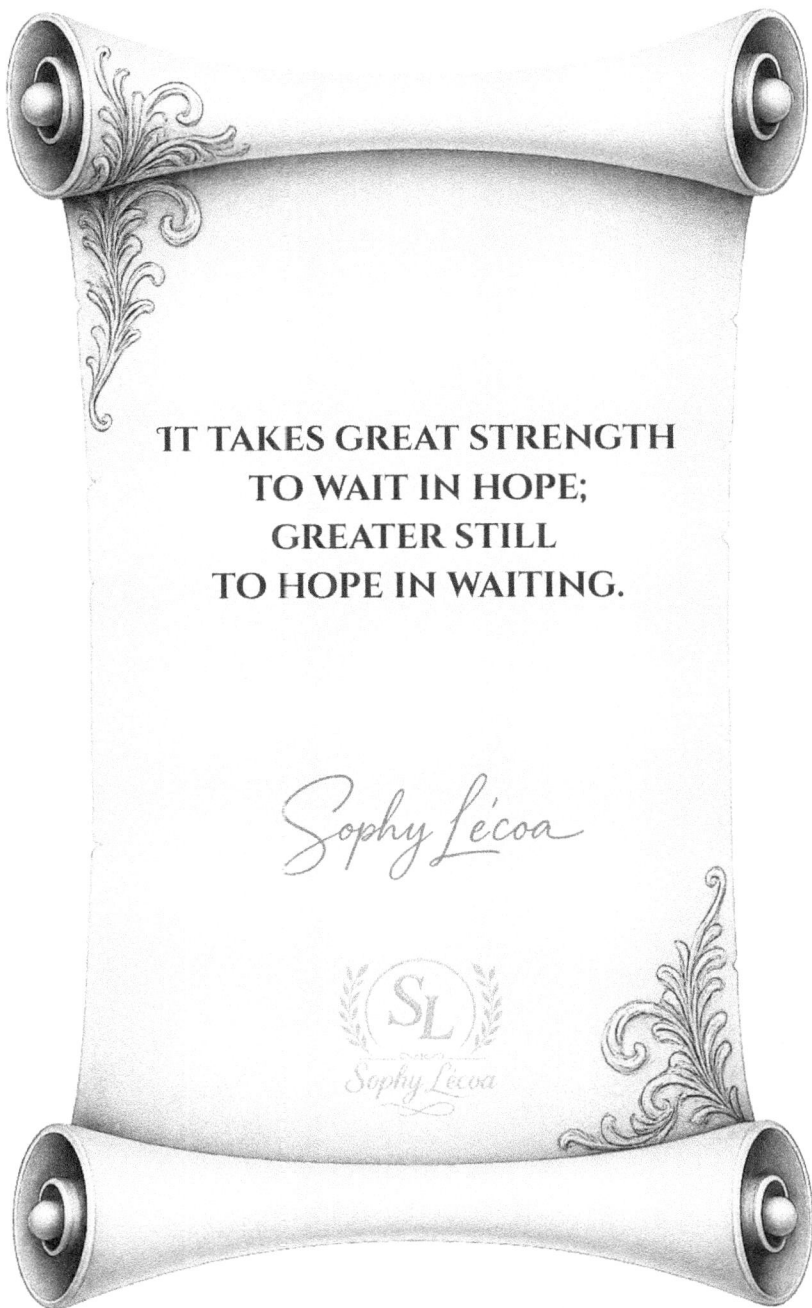

IT TAKES GREAT STRENGTH
TO WAIT IN HOPE;
GREATER STILL
TO HOPE IN WAITING.

Sophy Lécoa

Chapter 13

Mama's Medicine— Mamaia's Magic

"Between Mama's medicine and *Mamaia's* magic, I learned that healing didn't always taste sweet — but sometimes, it gave you hope enough to dream of sugar, and better days."

Two women, two worlds of healing.

One wore a crisp uniform and a badge of honor, walking the sterile halls of the Military Hospital where, from the High Commander to the last soldier, everyone knew her name. That was Mama — modern, disciplined, precise, admired by all.

The other moved in whispers and mystery, brewing remedies that looked like trouble in a jar, smelling of earth and secrets… yet working faster than any doctor's hand could promise. That was *Mamaia* — the healer.

And between them, there I was — a little girl watching two kinds of magic unfold. One that made men salute. One that made fevers vanish overnight. Even at eight years old, I wondered: which was stronger — the medicine in a syringe... or the kind you had to hold your breath to swallow?

A Sickness and a Spell

One rare day of sickness came like a sudden ambush — a stomach bug so fierce I could barely stop moaning. *Mamaia's* movements grew sharper, faster, like a field doctor in battle — no time for debate, no mercy for weak stomachs.

She prepared *legătura la burtă* (a mush of vegetables, herbs, vinegar, and corn flour). It looked like swamp mud, smelled like pickles rotting in the sun, and stung my eyes before it even touched me. I would have chosen death over letting it near me.

Mamaia did not care.

She slapped it onto my belly with the precision of a blacksmith striking iron, wrapped me tight in a towel, and began rubbing my arms, neck, and chest with a fiery liquid that burned like a hundred ants racing under my skin. The room filled with the scent of vinegar, garlic, and despair. My stomach churned harder just from the smell.

She sat beside me, eyes locked on mine, daring the sickness to fight her. One hand stroked my arm firmly under the blanket while her lips moved in a low whisper — half spell, half prayer. I caught only a few words; the rest was a murmur like a private meeting between her and God, plotting on my behalf. In her gaze was something rare: steady kindness.

Relief crept in like cautious footsteps. The pain loosened its grip. The nausea faded. Warmth spread through me like a slow sunrise after a storm.

"I knew it," Mamaia smirked. "Works even on a little devil like you."

I managed a weak laugh, secretly amazed it had worked. She checked my forehead with the pride of a witch doctor who had just won a war. For a moment, her eyes softened — a flicker of love that rarely made it past her rough hands.

Questions for Mamaia

That afternoon I drifted between naps, catching glimpses of her moving through the room, checking on me without words.

"Mamaia?" I called when she passed again.
"Feeling bad again?"
"No. Better. I just… want to ask you something."
She sighed. "Make it fast. I've got dinner to make."
"Do you think I could've died this time?"
"Nooo," she laughed, "little devils like you never die."
"One more question! When did Grandpa die?"
Her shoulders softened. "When your mama was young."
"How?"
"His heart just stopped. What your mama calls a heart attack."
"Couldn't you help him with *legătura la burtă*?"
"There was no time, Sophy. He just fell, and his heart

stopped."

"Are you afraid of death, *Mamaia?*"

She met my eyes, steady. "No. I can't wait to meet him in heaven."

"Are angry people going to heaven?"

"No. Just good people."

"Aren't you afraid they might not let you in?"

"Oh, they'll let me in," she said with quiet certainty. *"God knows my heart."*

And just like that, she smoothed her apron and went back to the kitchen, leaving me to wonder about death, heaven, and her mysterious kind of love.

Sugar, Laughter, and Better Days

By evening, the "hospital room" was dismantled. *Mamaia* scrubbed my belly clean, muttering about little devils who scare everyone half to death. At the table, she set plain white rice in front of me — the official aftermath food of healing, good for everything except disappointment.

"Rozi," she told Mama, "this Sunday we should take a little hike, all four of us. I want to show you more plants, more herbs — things you can use to make real medicine."

"That is a great idea, *Maicuța.*"

Mama's tired smile grew. "One of my patients promised to put aside sugar, oil, eggs, and flour for me — no lines, no waiting."

For a moment, the table stilled. In communist Romania, that wasn't just kindness — it was a miracle.

"That means flan whenever I want, Mama?" I gasped.

Mamaia's hands folded, her voice warm. "Then we'll have wild berry jams and sweet syrups stacked high this winter."

"I'll gather more berries this time," I announced. "And I won't eat them all!"

Clara snorted. "I'll believe that when I see it."

"Mamaaa…!" eyes pleading for her to defend me. *Mamaia* teased, "Clara is right. You'd rather do anything than learn to cook. God forbid you lift a spoon unless it's to taste."

"I don't need to cook," I grinned. "When I grow up, I'll have my own chef."

Mama raised an eyebrow. "And how will you pay her, Miss Professional Guest?"

"I'll take her everywhere I go. She'll cook for the whole family. We'll eat, laugh, and have fun together."

Mamaia lifted her hands to the ceiling. "Sweet Lord, have mercy on us. What kind of child is this?"

Laughter spilled around the table, weaving itself into the rare sweetness of that night — a promise of better days.

The Mountain

The days until Sunday dragged on far too slowly for my liking. I counted every hour, every minute, as if staring hard enough at the clock could make time move faster. But finally, Sunday came.

We packed our little backpacks carefully — sandwiches with *slăninuță*, apples, bottles of water, and all kinds of bags, cups, and baskets for the treasures of the forest we hoped to gather. I was the first one ready, shoes on, coat zipped, standing guard at the door like a soldier awaiting orders.

"Come on, let's go already!" I urged, hopping from one foot to the other.

Mama glanced at me, smiling softly as she buttoned her jacket. "Slow down, Sophy. You know *Măicuța's* legs have been hurting badly lately, remember?"

"Yes, I remember," I said quickly, turning to *Mamaia*, who was bent over, struggling with her boots. I bent down to help her. "But she told me, sometimes they hurt more, and sometimes less, right, *Mamaia*?" I looked at her for confirmation.

She let out a sharp sigh, half pain, half annoyance, and muttered, "Yes, Sophy… today is one of the 'more' days."

"Is it more more, or just a little more?" I pressed on, my curiosity refusing to rest.

Clara groaned and tugged at my sleeve. "Let's just go wait downstairs, Sophy. They don't have room to breathe. You'll get them dizzy with all your questions."

Mama chuckled. "That's actually a great idea. Go on, we'll be right there."

I tilted my head, confused. "Who exactly gets dizzy, Clara? *Mamaia*? She didn't look dizzy to me…"

Clara rolled her eyes and pushed me gently toward the stairs. "Trust me, Sophy… she's this close to being dizzy."

Behind us, *Mamaia* muttered under her breath, half-smiling despite herself, "This child could wear out a saint with that mouth of hers…"

It was a perfect sunny day, the kind that makes you wonder if the sky has ever been anything but blue. From the mountain, the view of the city and beyond stretched endlessly, every rooftop and winding street crystal clear in the distance. Not a single white cloud dared to touch the sky's infinite blue.

The air was alive with the gentle hum of bees and the chirping of birds, yet the hills themselves felt wrapped in a surreal calm, as if the world had decided to pause just for us.

Far behind, *Mamaia* and Mama walked slowly, stopping often as *Mamaia* pointed to plants, her voice spilling quiet wisdom, teaching and teaching like a devoted mentor to her eager apprentice.

Clara was a few steps ahead of me, whistling like the whole world belonged to her. I took a few exaggerated, noisy sips of air now and then, trying to catch up, trying to whistle along — but only spit came out, no sound. We laughed without words, our game unspoken and timeless.

For a moment, I stopped and looked back at *Mamaia*. She was only half a head taller than me now. A strange thought brushed over me: how small must I have been the day she first moved in with us, when she seemed like a giant? So much had changed since then. And today felt like another change was coming — not the heavy kind we had grown used to, but something lighter, brighter. A future filled with *Mamaia* smiling more, our cellar stacked high with good food, love finally blooming where worry had lived too long.

My thoughts were interrupted by a tug on my sleeve. "Let's scream," Clara said, eyes sparkling.

"Yes, let's do that."

We ran toward the edge of the mountain where *Brașov* lay open before us in all its quiet splendor. Arms stretched wide, lungs full, we screamed with everything we had. And in my mind, this time, that scream was more than just play — it was a wish, a command, a desperate attempt *to shatter the invisible spell of oppression* hanging over the city, over our family, over all families beneath that blazing sun.

That Sunday felt different — lighter, brighter, as if carrying a promise, I couldn't yet name.

~ ~ ~ ~ ~ ✧ ~ ~ ~ ~ ~

What Life Whispered to Me

There are moments when the world feels too heavy,
too silent,
too fixed in its sadness.

But a child's heart refuses that kind of weight.
It believes there is always a way to break the spell —
sometimes with questions that make adults shift in
their chairs,
sometimes with laughter that refuses to die,
and sometimes with a scream that rises higher than
fear itself.

That day on the mountain, I carried more than a
small backpack.
I carried Mama's quiet courage — the kind that walks
straight through cold corridors and makes men in
uniform stand taller.
I carried Mamaia's stubborn magic — the kind that
smells of storms, stings like fire, yet somehow leaves
you healed by morning.

From syringes to whispered prayers,
from sterile halls to jars of mystery,
they had both been telling me the same thing all

along:
healing isn't only for the body.

It's for the spirit — for the part of you that still dares
to believe in better days.

And that day, high above the city,
arms open, lungs full,
I let my voice fly like it had wings.

It wasn't just a game with Clara —
it was a wish, a command,
a defiance against the gray spell that had wrapped it-
self around our lives.

And I understood:
freedom is never handed to you.
It is something your soul is born knowing how to call
for —
again and again —
until the whole world finally listens.

— Sophy Le'coa

~ ~ ~ ~ ~ ✧ ~ ~ ~ ~ ~

WHEN HOPE HAS
NO WORDS OR PLANS —
THE SKY STILL HEARS
THE CRY FOR **TOMORROW.**

Sophy Lécoa

Chapter 14

A Confession and a Little Buzz

Sundays were Mama's days.

Museums, art galleries, theater plays — sometimes even a foreign movie we had to line up for since dawn just to have a seat. Clara and I would come home with the tickets clutched in our hands like they were golden keys to another world.

But when Mama worked a Sunday shift, *Mamaia* took over — and more often than not, that meant church.

One particular Sunday, she announced we'd be part of a special service this time.

"Confession Day," she said, tightening her scarf under her chin. "You go to the priest, you kneel, hands together, eyes down. Answer his questions. Nothing less, nothing more. Hear me?"

"Yes, *Mamaia*," we chimed in unison.

The church loomed like a castle when we arrived,

beautiful but heavy. Inside, the air was thick with candle smoke and incense, the scent of wax and something older, holy. People stood so close we brushed shoulders, every woman with a scarf over her head — a quiet rule of respect in the house of God.

The walls were alive with color, *icoane* painted right on the stone, saints watching from every corner. Even the narrow-stained windows looked like guards on duty, standing tall and solemn.

At the front, the priest appeared in a robe of gold, patterned with sacred symbols, his tall hat glinting in the dim light. Something about him made the air shimmer, as if he wasn't quite of this earth. *Mamaia* found us a spot, declared it "just right," and we stood like statues waiting for the sermon.

When it began, silence dropped like a weight. The priest read in a voice that didn't sound quite human — half chant, half command — and every few moments the entire room sank to its knees, made the sign of the cross, then rose again. *Mamaia* groaned under her breath with each motion, her knees not what they used to be, but she soldiered on.

It went on like that for what felt like forever. I could hear my blood swishing in my ears from all the quiet.

Finally, confession began.

A long, slow line formed. I thought bitterly, *even talking to God, you need to queue up. I hope He's not communist too.*

Mamaia went first, kneeling, the priest draping a long golden cloth over her head like a curtain of power.

They whispered back and forth, then he fed her a sip of something from a small, ornate silver chalice. She made the sign of the cross, serious as ever, and shuffled back to us, nudging Clara
forward.

Clara copied every move perfectly, like she'd been practicing all week. My turn came next. I already knew the drill — kneel, hands clasped, head bowed. Easy.

"What's your name, my daughter?" the priest asked softly.
"I'm Sophy."
"Sophy," he said, voice deep and slow, "tell the Heavenly Father everything you've done wrong, so He can forgive you and make you clean."

I peeked up, frowning. "I didn't do anything wrong. Only good and beautiful things." I said it firmly, *because that was my truth.*

The corner of his mouth twitched, but he stayed solemn. "Are you sure, Sophy?"
"Yes," I nodded, then spun halfway around, pointing. "You can ask Clara."

He chuckled quietly, his hand pressing gently on my head to turn me back. "Who else is here with you?"
"*Mamaia,*" I said quickly.
"Should we ask *Mamaia* if there's anything you might've forgotten?"

I glanced back. *Mamaia* was staring at the floor, cheeks flushed red, her hands clamped together so tight they looked like knotted rope.

"I think…" I whispered conspiratorially, "she's too busy talking to God right now."

The priest stifled a laugh, muttered a blessing over me, then solemnly said, "In the name of the Father, the Son, and the Holy Spirit."

I stood, relieved, and at last received my mysterious sip from the grand silver cup. It tasted strange — sweet and bitter at once — but not bad. Later I learned it was wine.

We waited quietly for the closing prayer when it hit me — heat rising through my belly, a giddy warmth spreading all the way to my fingertips. I glanced at Clara. She looked dazed, dreamy, like her head was full of honey.

We locked eyes. That was it.

The giggles started small, bubbling up like soda fizz, shoulders shaking as we tried to keep our heads bowed. But the harder we tried to stop, the worse it got. My stomach cramped from holding in the laugh, and tears blurred my eyes. Clara was no better, biting her lip, face cherry red.

Every pious head turned, staring at us with scandalized silence. I risked one look at *Mamaia*. Her glare could have frozen fire. And that did it — Clara snorted out loud, and I followed, laughter bursting like a dam breaking.

People parted as if we carried a plague, making a narrow path straight to the door. We stumbled out into the sunlight, doubled over with helpless, breathless laughter.

That was the last time *Mamaia* took us to church with her.

Turns out, one little spoonful of wine was enough to make a memory that would last forever.

Even now, I still don't believe that talking to God should pass through someone else. That day in church didn't teach me guilt or confession — it taught me that my heart already knew how to speak to Him, without a middleman, without a script.
And even as a little girl with wine on my tongue and giggles in my chest,
I knew one thing for sure:
God and I — we had a direct line.*

And somewhere deep down, in a place I couldn't yet name, I felt the first small stirring of a truth that would return to me years later in a far greater way:

No system built by man — whether in faith, in politics, or in the rules of an entire nation — should ever stand between me, God and the freedom to speak for myself. — Sophy Le'coa

~ ~ ~ ~ ~ ✧ ~ ~ ~ ~ ~

What Life Whispered to Me

*Holiness doesn't always stand frozen in perfect
silence.
Sometimes it tastes like mystery, warms you like a secret fire,
and sends you tumbling out the church doors
with laughter you can't quite contain.*

*That day, I learned faith isn't measured
by the heaviness of rules or the strictness of rituals,
but by the freedom with which your soul dares to
speak to its Maker.*

*No line, no middleman, no whispered list of sins
could ever make Him love me more —
and no ritual could make my heart belong to Him
less.*

*And someday, I'd learn the same was true
for every voice worth raising in this world.*

— Sophy Le'coa

~ ~ ~ ~ ~ ✧ ~ ~ ~ ~ ~

GOD NEVER NEEDED A
MIDDLEMAN —
ONLY THE FREEDOM OF A
LAUGHING SOUL.

Sophy Lécoa

Chapter 15

Little Orange Bear

That day had ended in giggles and whispers to God.
I didn't know that somewhere ahead, life was holding a
different kind of prayer — one only a child could understand.

Late fall came dressed in heavy gray, the kind that
pressed on your eyelids and slowed your feet. The streets
glistened with leftover rain, puddles stretched thin and
cracked like old glass under my dragging shoes. My legs
ached, my stomach grumbled, and my head still buzzed from
endless tests at school — questions, numbers, handwriting
drills, all blurring together like a swarm of bees I couldn't
escape.

Normally, gymnastics practice was my refuge, the one
place my body felt light and free. But that Wednesday, instead
of the usual two hours, our coach kept us for three — pushing
harder, barking counts louder, until every muscle in me

burned and trembled. By the time we were dismissed, I'd left every drop of energy on the mat.

I trudged home under the dimming sky, too tired to care about splashing through puddles, too hungry to think of anything but the bread and butter I'd forgotten to pack that morning. My backpack felt heavier than it should — not from books, but from the weight of homework waiting for me, a mountain of tasks that would stretch late into the night, lit only by stubborn flickers of candlelight.

It was nearly dark when I reached the corner near our block. A few lampposts stood like weary sentinels, casting weak halos of light.

Clara was there, waiting, her eyes holding a touch of worry. Usually, seeing her made the day's heaviness lift. But that night, even her smile couldn't chase the tiredness away. She didn't ask anything — just gave me that soft, wordless smile, took my backpack from my shoulders, and walked beside me in quiet understanding.

Then, out of nowhere, it happened.

Ramona, our neighbor from the second floor, had spotted us from her window. She rushed outside, her face alight with excitement. She had received a package from Germany.

In communist Romania, those packages were rare treasures — tiny windows into a forbidden world, bursting with colors and promises.

From her hands, Ramona held out a small box that looked ordinary to anyone else but was pure magic to us.

Inside, nestled like jewels, were gummy bears — bright, shiny, and smelling faintly of some faraway summer. We stared at them, wide-eyed, as though they were alive.

"Pick one each," Ramona said warmly.

We froze. Choosing just one from that miracle felt almost like casting a spell.

I chose orange. Clara chose yellow.

The moment I placed mine on my tongue, the world stopped.

The sweetness… the fruit… the softness… it was unlike anything I'd ever tasted.

But I didn't eat it. Not yet.

That orange bear became mine —

my secret,

my talisman.

I kept it wrapped inside a tiny pouch, hidden from sight. Each night, I would take it out, peel the wrapper back slowly so its little head wouldn't tear, hold it in my palm, inhale its foreign sweetness. Sometimes I'd place it in my mouth for just a moment — not to chew, only to feel it there — before tucking it away again.

For months, I guarded that gummy bear as though it held the key to something larger. And maybe it did. It shrank over time, but still, somehow, it remained a bear.

One day, without warning, I knew it was time.
I placed it whole on my tongue, closed my eyes, and let it dissolve slowly, every drop of flavor sinking deep inside me. I savored it until nothing remained.

And when it was gone, I didn't cry.
Because it had never been just candy.

It was a promise.

Proof that somewhere — beyond the lines, the cold, the gray silence — there was a world that tasted like freedom.

Even now, when I bite into a gummy bear, I pause. I close my eyes.
And the child in me stirs, smiles, and remembers she once dreamed.

~ ~ ~ ~ ~ ✧ ~ ~ ~ ~ ~

What Life Whispered to Me

Sometimes, the smallest gifts leave the deepest traces.
An orange gummy bear… a piece of candy… a fleet-
ing burst of flavor —
can open the door to an entire world.

For me, that world was called America.
In my childhood, freedom had no face.
But it had a taste.
A color.
And the shape of a soft, glowing bear.

Life whispered to me then that joy isn't measured by
how much you hold in your hands,
but by how deeply you feel it in your heart.
That some things don't need to last forever
to leave an eternal mark.

It also whispered that hope hides in the most unex-
pected places —
in a bag of sweets,
in a simple act of generosity,
in a quiet evening when the world feels gray
but your soul begins to glow.

And most of all...
that sometimes, your biggest dream can begin with
something so small —
a tiny orange bear resting in your palm —
and yet carry the weight of a promise big enough to
change your life.

Because the same way my heart once learned it could
speak to God without a middleman,
it also learned it could dream without permission.

That freedom doesn't wait for gates to open —
sometimes, it slips quietly into your hands,
sweet, bright, and unexpected...
like a single orange bear that told me,
long before I knew the word for it,
what liberty tasted like.

— Sophy Le'coa

~ ~ ~ ~ ~ ✧ ~ ~ ~ ~ ~

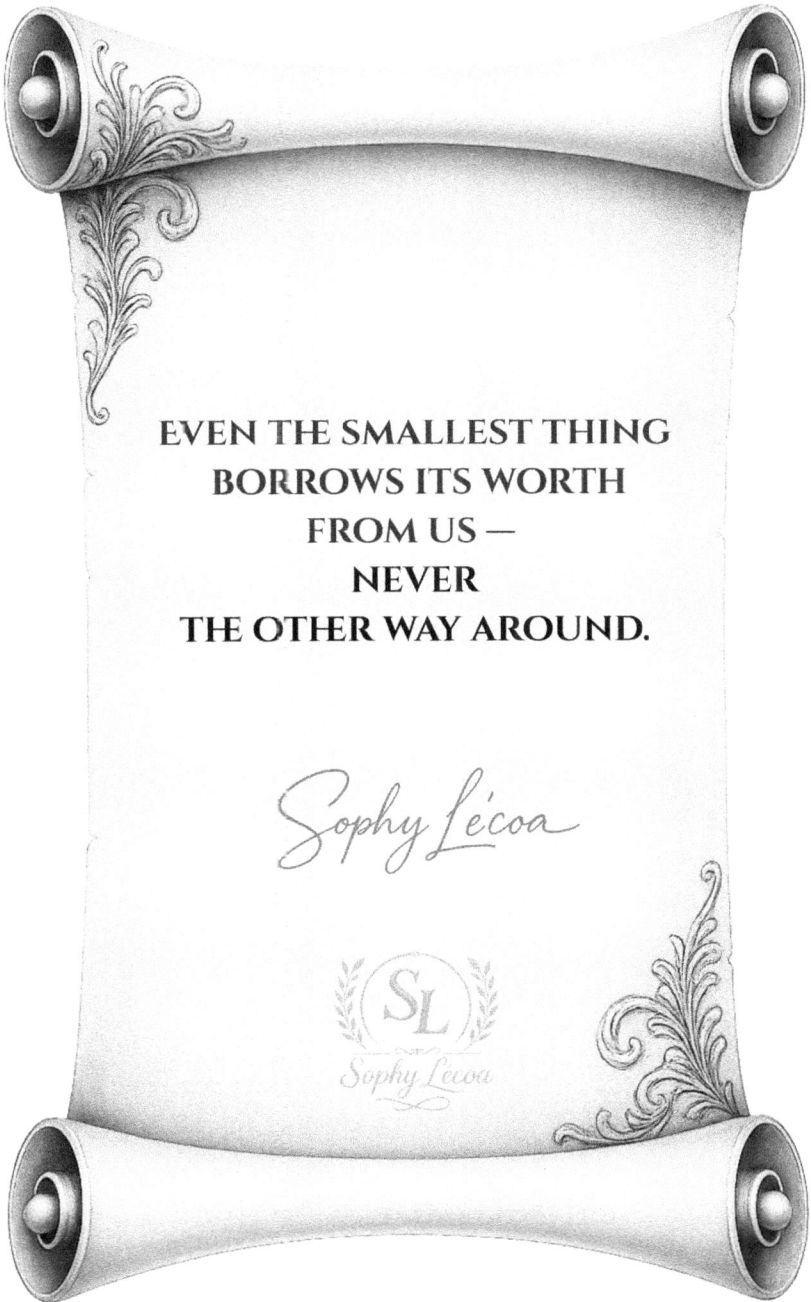

EVEN THE SMALLEST THING
BORROWS ITS WORTH
FROM US —
NEVER
THE OTHER WAY AROUND.

Sophy Lécoa

Chapter 16

First Change

Winter came that year with more than snow.
It crept into our home like a silent intruder, settling not only on rooftops and windowsills but deep in *Mamaia's* bones. First her legs ached, then her back, and soon it seemed every part of her body whispered of pain. She spent more time lying in bed, her naps stretching longer, her voice calling us less often. Even her usual scolding—sharp as a whip, part of the rhythm of our days—faded, leaving the house strangely quiet, as if a bell that once rang every hour had been forgotten.

Clara and I picked up more chores without a word. We scrubbed and swept, carried baskets of damp laundry to the little washing machine that rattled like an angry kettle, though Mama mostly washed by hand to save on power— "like the *dear leader* says," she'd mutter, half-mocking, half-cautious, her eyes darting toward the window as if even the walls had ears.

Cooking became more frequent too, though my clumsy hands often slowed the process more than they sped it up. Still, somehow, I was always branded the rebellious one, even when I tried to do good.

One late afternoon, Mamaia's voice floated softly from her room. It sounded weaker than I had ever heard it. "Sophy," she called, "please… come massage my back with this ointment."

I stepped in quietly. The room smelled of winter air slipping through the cracked window frame, mingled with the pungent, medicinal balm she held out to me. My stomach turned; I didn't want that sticky stuff on my hands. But I bit down on the thought, took the tin, and climbed onto the bed beside her.

"Here," she guided me, her voice fragile but precise. "A little more to the left, Sophy… yes… now higher. Slow, slow… like that."

When I finished, I held my fingers awkwardly in the air, slick and glistening with the ointment, trying not to grimace. I was about to wipe them clean when I noticed her eyes shimmering with tears.

My heart sank. My hands fell to my lap. I forgot about the smell, the stickiness, everything.

"*Mamaia*… why are you crying? Is it the pain?" I whispered.

She shook her head slowly, her lips trembling. "No, Sophy. It feels better now. Your hands…" Her voice broke. "Your hands are like an angel's hands."

Something inside me shifted — a new weight pressing down on my chest, both heavy and light at once. *Mamaia* had never spoken to me like that before — never compared me to something so tender, so divine.

"Then why are you crying? You make me wanna cry." I said, my own tears brimming.

She turned her gaze toward the wall, as if her memories had been painted there long ago.
"Because I miss my home, Sophy. I miss the fresh air of my village, my garden, my cow *Steluța*... oh, she gave the sweetest milk, you can't imagine. She was such a good cow. The neighbors, the hills, the meadows..." Her voice cracked again. "*Steluța* had a white star on her forehead, shining every morning when I went to milk her. Oh, how I loved her."

A bittersweet heaviness filled me. I swiped a tear before it could fall.
"Tell me more, *Mamaia*." I said softly, leaning closer as if I could pull her stories out of her heart.

"I'm tired now, Sophy," she whispered. "I'll tell you more later."
"You promise?"
Her lips curved into a faint, trembling smile. "I promise."

I left the room slowly, no longer caring how my hands smelled. My mind was full of questions I couldn't stop. Why hadn't she spoken to me like this before? Was it pain that stripped away all the walls people build around their hearts? Was kindness buried deep inside us, waiting for the body to break before it could surface?

That day marked something quiet but unshakable — a change in me, a silent tide rising inside my young soul, reshaping what I thought love looked like.

From then on, it became a ritual.

Daily, *Mamaia* seemed slower, her naps longer, her voice quieter. But the "treatments" became our secret bridge. I'd grab the ointment and ask, "Do you want a massage, *Mamaia*?" She would nod with a small smile.

"Yes, Sophy. God bless you and your little hands," she'd say. Every time, my heart swelled with a strange joy. I started adding more to my massages, rubbing her arms and hands, hoping to chase away every ounce of pain.

"Tell me about your mama," I asked one evening, my fingers tracing slow circles on her palms.

"She came from a long line of healers," *Mamaia* said softly. "She lived in a neighboring village, kind and wise… everyone came to her for help."

I listened, mesmerized, as she painted pictures of a woman I had never met but could almost see — stories of old remedies, nights under starlight, laughter echoing in fields where freedom was not a dream but a way of life.

She even retold children's tales like *Capra cu trei iezi* (The Goat with Three Kids), adding twists I had never heard before, changing endings, filling them with color, joy, and victories. Time vanished when she spoke, as if her words stretched the evening into something sacred.

One night, curious, I whispered, "What were you like as a little girl?"

Her eyes lit up with a fleeting spark. "Full of life—just like you, Sophy."

In that moment, a quiet promise took root in my heart: I would never wait until my body broke to be kind to others. I would let my good words escape while there was still time.

She went on, voice growing lighter as memories carried her away. "We felt free, running with our animals, playing until dark. A piece of bread and a cup of milk could feed a whole day's joy. I only went to school for two years… boys were given more. Times changed some things for better, others for worse." Her gaze grew distant. "I pray to Almighty God that it will keep changing for the better — for you, for your mama, for everyone."

And then she recited, almost singing, a verse from Revelation 21:4:

"He will wipe every tear from their eyes.
There will be no more death or mourning or crying or pain,
for the old order of things has passed away."

She closed her eyes. "Always believe in Jesus, Sophy. He is the truth, the way, and the light."

Those moments weren't just stories. *They were a hand reaching from the past, passing down a faith unbroken by time or sorrow.* It wasn't if the world would change — it was when. My heart grew lighter, full of quiet, fierce expectation.

With every "treatment," *Mamaia* seemed to glow a little from within. I saw not just an old woman in pain, but a child who once ran free, a mother who once loved deeply, a soul that knew eternal truths by heart.

Mama handled the medicines and injections I couldn't bear to watch, while I offered warmth and listening ears.

Sometimes, when *Mamaia* drifted to sleep, I'd sit there silently, holding her hand, feeling a strange kind of holiness fill the room.

Eventually, *Mamaia* went to the hospital for a while, though nothing more could really be done.
Looking back, I think she was ready — to live free of pain and sorrow, to watch over us from heaven, just as she said she would, eternally.

~ ~ ~ ~ ~ ✧ ~ ~ ~ ~ ~

What Life Whispered to Me

Pain has a strange way of peeling us back to the
truth.
It strips away our armor, our sharp words, our hur-
ried tones,
until only the tender parts of us remain.

I learned this while rubbing ointment into my grand-
mother's aching back,
watching her tears spill not from pain,
but from longing —
longing for her home, for a cow with a star on its fore-
head,
for fields that once smelled of freedom.

And I wondered — why do we wait for pain to make
us gentle?
Why do we hold back our kindest words,
the ones that could soften a soul,
until time threatens to run out?
Why does it take the breaking of the body
for the beauty of the heart to finally speak?

That day I made myself a promise:
I will not wait for life to strip me bare before I love

openly.

If my words can be healing, I will speak them now.
If my hands can soothe, I will not hesitate to reach out.
If kindness can live in me, it should not need sorrow to set it free.

Mamaia's stories left more than memories.
They left me with a truth I still carry:
love that is buried deep inside serves no one.
A heart that holds back its gentleness is like a garden never watered —
its flowers die unseen.

Pain may force the blossoms out,
but why not let them grow in the sunlight of ordinary days?

And then came a deeper whisper,
one I didn't fully understand at that age
but felt in my bones:

life is fleeting,
but love and faith are not.

They pass from one soul to another,
like a torch in the dark,
like verses learned by heart and never forgotten.

They survive the grayness of a world that hurts,
the silence of years,
even death itself.

If there is a truth that aches to be known, it is this:
every touch,
every word of kindness,
every prayer said with belief
carries a piece of eternity in it.

We may think they are small, fleeting gestures,
but they are not.

They are the only treasures we truly leave behind —
the echoes of love that no winter can bury.

So now I try, even when I fail,
to live by the promise I made as a child
with ointment on my hands:

let the good in me slip out before pain has to set it
free.

For one day,
we will all long for someone's garden,
someone's voice,
someone's light.

And only the love we dared to give
will remain to warm the air we leave behind.

— Sophy Le'coa

~ ~ ~ ~ ~ ✧ ~ ~ ~ ~ ~

LET YOUR GOODNESS
FLOW FREELY —
DON'T WAIT
FOR PAIN'S HARSH
OBLIVION.

Sophy Lécoa

Chapter 17

Drops of Heaven

By spring, *Mamaia* could no longer rise from bed.
Her stories, once spilling into every corner of the house, faded
into a silence so deep it felt like a missing heartbeat. The house
itself began to change — no longer the steady rhythm of ordinary days, but a kind of train station, with footsteps coming
and going, voices softened to whispers, and eyes that carried
news without words.

Visitors arrived with arms full of food. Loaves of bread,
jars of preserves, pots of steaming soup — so much that our
old fridge seemed to groan under the weight. The smell of
warm bread and boiled vegetables clung to the air, but it
could not sweeten the heaviness that had settled in our rooms.

Mama moved among the visitors like a pale shadow —
serving tea, nodding politely, her lips forming practiced
smiles that never reached her eyes. Every so often she would
slip into *Mamaia's* room, lean close, and whisper something

against her forehead, her hand resting there just a moment longer than necessary, as if sealing a blessing only the two of them understood.

Clara and I kept near each other, speaking little. We didn't need words; the silence between us had its own language. Beneath it, one thought pulsed in both our minds — the Promise.

The one I had once made Clara swear to keep.

The one I now prayed would never need to be kept.

The room where *Mamaia* lay was bright with flowers in vases, but beauty could not lift the weight from the air. I would have traded every cooked meal, every mended hem, every clean floor she had ever given us for just one more story, one more memory pulled from her youth before the well went dry.

Then the silence broke.

A thud. A rush of footsteps. Voices sharp with panic.

Clara and I ran toward the sound.

Mama lay on the living room floor, her body twisted, her skin pale. Miss Greta, Mama's closest friend and head nurse at the hospital, was already on her knees, cradling Mama's head.

"Mama!" My voice tore out of me. I dropped to the floor, reaching for her hand.

"She has no pulse," Miss Greta said quietly, her eyes flicking up to mine with a weight that nearly stopped my own heart.

"No, no, no…" Clara's voice broke beside me. Tears blurred my vision.

In my mind flashed the image of Grandpa's lifeless body on the couch. Not again. Please, not again.

But Mama was still whispering.

Her lips moved, trembling, speaking words only Miss Greta could hear — about us, about what to do in case…

I froze.

If she had no pulse, how could she still speak?

The air seemed to hold its breath.

"Yes, Rozy… I'm here," Miss Greta murmured, her voice trembling. Then suddenly, her eyes widened. "Her pulse is back."

Relief hit me so hard it made me dizzy. My sobs came out in a rush, and I clung to Mama's hand as if I could anchor her here by sheer will.

"Sophy, Clara," Miss Greta said firmly, "go wait for the ambulance. Guide them up the moment they arrive."

We ran down the stairs, hearts hammering, prayers spilling from our lips into the spring air. Clara held me close, whispering, "Shh… she'll be fine," though her own voice was shaking.

The ambulance arrived, red lights slicing through the daylight. Hope surged like a sharp breath. We led the medics upstairs, their heavy steps echoing off the narrow walls.

The stretcher wouldn't fit, so they wrapped Mama in a blanket and carried her carefully. One shoe slipped from her foot on the way down, her bare heel pale against the stair-well's worn stone. Miss Greta kept pace with them, speaking softly into Mama's ear, urging her to hold on.

At the doorway, Clara and I stopped.

We watched the red-and-white ambulance pull away, carrying the one woman who held our lives together. The sound of its siren faded into the distance, leaving only the throb of our hearts in the quiet street.

That same evening, Aunt Vio came and gently took *Mamaia* to the countryside — the place she had longed for, her home, her hills, her cow with the star-shaped mark on its forehead. It felt like opening the sky for a bird one last time.

Miss Gabi, Mama's other close friend, came to stay with us. She assured us Mama was strong, that she was in the best hands, that everything would be alright. I clung to her words. To Clara's whispered reassurances.
They were like drops of heaven — small, pure, and enough to keep my heart beating through the night.

And when sleep finally came, it came in Clara's arms, where the world felt warm again, if only for a little while.

~ ~ ~ ~ ~ ✧ ~ ~ ~ ~ ~

What Life Whispered to Me

Some truths only reveal themselves in the quiet after-
math of a gasp.

That night — when the one who held our whole
world collapsed before us — I didn't just feel fear.
I felt a veil lifting Something holy and incomprehen-
sible brushed past the edges of what I thought I un-
derstood.

I had known since I was three years old that the line
between life and death is razor-thin.
One breath, one moment — and Daddy was gone for-
ever.

But this time, the rules bent.
This time, Mama had no pulse... and still, she whis-
pered.
Still, she spoke of us — of what to do in case she
didn't return.
She was, by every measure, already leaving... and yet
she remained, loving, holding on, anchored to us by
something unseen.

It made no sense.

And yet, it made something else: faith.

That night, I stopped wondering if God was real.
Not because of a verse, not because of a sermon — but
because of a miracle I saw unfold in front of me.
Because what else could explain a voice speaking from
a body with no pulse?
What else could carry her back to us — not science,
not chance, but mercy?

From that moment on, I understood: Heaven doesn't
always open with grand gestures.
Sometimes it opens in the small, unshakable details —
in a shoe slipping off a foot,
in a nurse's whisper,
in the quiet return of a pulse when no one expects it.

I also learned that love doesn't need to shout to be
powerful.
It lives in the repetition of a sister's voice, speaking
the same promise again and again until her belief be-
comes your lifeline.
It breathes in the soft eyes of a family friend who be-
comes your anchor without asking.
It surrounds you like a second skin, in arms that
tremble but do not let go.

We imagine miracles to be loud.
But some arrive like dew — soft, quiet, undeniable.

So if you ever find yourself standing on that invisible
line between what was and what might be —
don't panic. Don't run.
Just listen.

Sometimes Heaven is closer than you think.
And sometimes, the ones we think are gone… are not
gone at all.
Not yet.

— Sophy Le'coa

~ ~ ~ ~ ~ ✧ ~ ~ ~ ~ ~

THERE ARE MOMENTS
IN LIFE
WHEN DOUBT DISSOLVES,
AND THE QUESTION
OF GOD'S EXISTENCE
FALLS SILENT —
BECAUSE DEEP INSIDE,
YOU ALREADY KNOW.

Sophy Lécoa

Chapter 18

The Cat with Seven Lives

The next morning, we woke up to good news.
Mama was alive.

At only thirty-five years old, she had suffered a heart
attack —
the kind that could take anyone. But not her. Not *Rozi*.
She had slipped in and out of this world once more, baffling
the doctors.
Her heart paused again in the early hours, and again she
returned.

By morning, she stabilized.
From that day forward, the nurses began calling her *Pisica cu
şapte vieţi* —
The Cat with Seven Lives.

Miss Gabi, Mama's best friend and guardian angel

during those days, stayed with us in the apartment. She gave us updates like lullabies — gentle, reassuring. She treated us with the same warmth she always had, but even her voice, soft as it was, couldn't wash away the fear rising in my chest.

I didn't want to lose Mama.

Not now.

Not later.

Not ever.

Clara sensed it too. She was quieter than usual, as if her thoughts had turned into heavy stones. Then one day, she turned to me.

"Sophy," she said. "Let's promise we'll take care of Mama."

"I promise," I replied without hesitation. "I promise with all my heart."

Another silence passed between us, one of those sacred kinds that needs no explaining. Then Clara spoke again. "Sophy, promise we'll help Mama more."

"I promise," I said again. "We'll help her more. Always."

And just like that, we made a covenant. Not with words alone, but with the aching hearts of two little girls who had already seen too much.

Those days felt like the house had forgotten how to echo laughter.

It was as if the walls had soaked in all our joy and replaced it with waiting.

Then, at the end of that long week, came the news.

Mamaia passed away.

Peacefully.

Surrounded by family.

In the village she loved, in the air she had longed for, far from the pain that had bound her.

Clara and I looked at each other.

No words.

But the same thought.

The Promise.

She had fulfilled it.

She had kept her word.

And now she was gone.

It hurt more than we knew how to say.

Mama was still recovering.

But grief doesn't wait for permission.

The doctors had made themselves clear:

— "No stress."

— "No rushing."

— "No heavy lifting."

— "Absolutely no exertion."

But how could she not go?

How could she not say goodbye to the woman who birthed her?

So, Mama rose.

She dressed.

She walked.

She stood tall at the graveside like a soldier, though we knew her body was anything but strong.

Clara and I never took our eyes off her.

Not once.

We watched her face.

Her hands.

Her breathing.

Every moment felt fragile, like one wrong breath would send her crashing again.

But she didn't fall.

She stood.

And with her — we stood too.

Shaken.

Changed.

But still whole.

Still a family.

After the funeral, there was no pause.

No quiet.

No rest.

The doctors pleaded again:

— "You need to stop."

— "Please take care of yourself."

But how could she?

We needed her.

So, she got up before the sun.

Tied her scarf.

Put on her old boots.

She walked the hills with her heart still fragile,

picking berries for jam,

gathering herbs for healing,

mushrooms for soup.

She came home with bags full of life,
while her body held barely enough strength to carry itself.
And never — not once — did I hear her complain.
She never asked, "Why me?"
She never broke in front of us.

She just kept going.
Like a quiet force of nature.
Like someone who knew there was no other way.

~ ~ ~ ~ ~ ✧ ~ ~ ~ ~ ~

What Life Whispered to Me

Some mothers love with words.
And some love with actions.
My mother loved with everything she had —
even when there was nothing left to give.

Life whispered to me then:
True love doesn't raise its voice.
It doesn't beg for recognition.
It doesn't pause to count the cost.

True love walks uphill
with blistered feet
and a heart barely holding together —
and still reaches the top.

I learned that a tired heart
can echo louder than a crowd.
That real strength isn't only in enduring,
but in rising —
again and again —
even when you know
you might fall.

And most of all, I learned:
Not all heroes wear capes

or carry swords of light.
Some rise at dawn
with swollen ankles and an aching chest,
gather berries, carry heavy baskets,
and whisper into the quiet:
"I'm still here.
I will keep going.
For you."

And somewhere in those whispers,
I realized —
love, like faith, doesn't need a middleman.
Her strength was its own prayer.
Her breath, its own altar.
And between her heart and God's,
there was only
a direct line.

— Sophy Le'coa

~ ~ ~ ~ ~ ✦ ~ ~ ~ ~ ~

SOME HEARTS
DO NOT BREAK —
THEY BEND INTO LOVE,
INTO SERVICE,
INTO SOMETHING SACRED.

Sophy Lécoa

Chapter 19

The Time We Became Equal

I was nine and a half when everything shifted.

It wasn't just Mama who changed.

Clara changed.

I changed.

Mama became more serious.

More precise.

Her time with us shrank into narrow slivers between work, rest, and endless responsibilities.

Her voice took on a new sharpness — her requests more like instructions, her presence more like a general in the war of daily survival.

Clara, determined to help, clung to the promise we made — but she wielded it like a sword.

Where there were once gentle nudges, there were now scoldings.

And fights.

Serious ones.

We used to bicker in silly ways, annoying Mama with our mischief.

But now, Clara fought to maintain control.

Her fuse was short.

Her eyes sharp.

The smallest misstep from me could ignite her fury.

I, too, changed.

I became quieter.

More inward.

I started thinking ahead before I spoke.

I asked myself questions no child should have to ask:

Will this upset Mama?

Will this make Clara angry?

Why does it feel like I'm wrong even when I'm trying my best?

It was a slow transition.

But it hurt.

A piece of my childhood vanished with Mamaia.

And nothing felt the same again.

We no longer played outside with the other children. Their laughter in the courtyard felt like echoes from another life.

In our world, school had taken over — demanding, endless, and hard.

Mama wanted more for us.

She hired tutors — mathematics, grammar, science — so we could one day escape.

"Tomorrow, we have math tutoring," Clara would murmur, head resting on a textbook.

"And grammar the day after," I'd sigh.

"Don't sigh, Sophy. Mama will hear."

"But I miss playing…"

She wouldn't answer.

She'd just squeeze my hand.

And in that little gesture, we gave each other patience.

Mama's eyes were always firm:

"Girls, you must grind hard. Studying is your only escape."

"Escape from what, Mama?" I once asked.

"From everything that's too heavy here. Study to get a good job. Be a nurse. A doctor. Something better."

"But Mama, you're a nurse. And it's still hard."

She paused.

Startled.

"Life dealt me a heavy hand," she whispered. "But yours can be different."

I almost replied — but Clara kicked my shin under the table.

That kick meant: Don't stress her.

That was one of our promises.

So, I stayed quiet.

Watching the candle flicker in the dark.

Everything had changed — except that little flame.

I wanted to be somewhere else — to run until I touched the horizon, to find a small door and go through it, and keep running until I reached America.

I wanted to be free, to breathe freely, and to say out loud I love America — without fearing the regime's consequences.

I wanted to send back huge packages of everything Mama needed.

And money.

So much money that Mama would never have to worry again.

Then I started thinking more about God.

About *Mamaia*.

About Jesus.

I wondered: Did God come to Mama? Or was He already in her, whispering?

If the body dies, and the lips are still, then it must be the spirit that moved her lips.

So if Mama's spirit remained to move her lips in whisper, it had to be divine.

Part of God.

Which meant... we all have it too.

And then I wondered about Clara.

Why was she so rough with me lately?

We still giggled and whispered at night.

But I had become cautious.

Tiptoeing around certain topics.

Afraid of saying the wrong thing.

I couldn't yet see how desperately she was trying to protect both me and Mama.

She didn't know how to carry it all.

We were just kids.

Now Mama was up every morning at 4 a.m. — cooking meals, heading to work, coming back for a few hours, only to leave again for *garda* — the dreaded night shift.

And Clara held the rest of the household together.

Back then, it didn't always feel like we were on the same team.

She was taller.

Stronger.

Quick to push kids away if they came too close to me.

My protector.

My bodyguard.

And my rival.

Every time I tried to speak up, she silenced me.

Every time I had an idea, she had a better one.

We fought like wild animals.

And she always won.

Always.

Until one day.

I was ten years old — old enough to know I couldn't stay the little one forever.

The fight started over something small.

A word.

A choice.

A clash of wills.

But I didn't back down.

I don't remember the details — just the heat in my chest.

The fire that said: No more.

And then it happened.

For the first time ever — I won.

We stood there, breathless.

Shocked.

The silence after the storm was thick — but not scary.

It felt… sacred.

Like something had just shifted.

Clara's eyes met mine.

And a grin tugged at her lips.

I grinned back.

Without words, we made a new promise:

No more sister-rankings.

No more thrones.

From that moment on — we were equals.

Best friends.

Confidants.

Two girls, side by side, ready to face the world.

Not because one was stronger.

But because we were finally back on the same side.

And even now, looking back — I know:

That was the day I didn't just gain my sister back.

I freed her from a burden she should've never had to carry.

I gained my voice back — and my best friend for life.

~ ~ ~ ~ ~ ✧ ~ ~ ~ ~ ~

What Life Whispered to Me

Sometimes, childhood doesn't end with age —
it ends when responsibility arrives too early,
when innocence is asked to carry weight.

For me, childhood ended with silence.
Not the peaceful kind,
but the silence that comes when you're afraid to speak
your truth,
afraid to upset the ones you love,
afraid of being one more burden on a mother who al-
ready gave too much.

But in that silence, something else grew:
A deeper noticing.
I learned to study expressions instead of explanations.
To understand what wasn't said.
To measure peace by the softness in my sister's hand
and the flicker of candlelight after Mama's shift.

When the world outside was gray, I dreamed in color.
When there was no room for joy, I made space inside
myself.
When freedom was forbidden, I whispered it in my

mind —

in English, in hope, in secret.

And I understood something precious:
Sometimes, the greatest strength isn't being loud, or
brave, or seen.
It's quietly choosing love when everything around
you feels like pressure.
It's promising to care, to help, to stay —
not because you're asked, but because your heart can't
do anything else.

Even in the quietest childhood,
a soul can awaken — and choose light.

— Sophy Le'coa

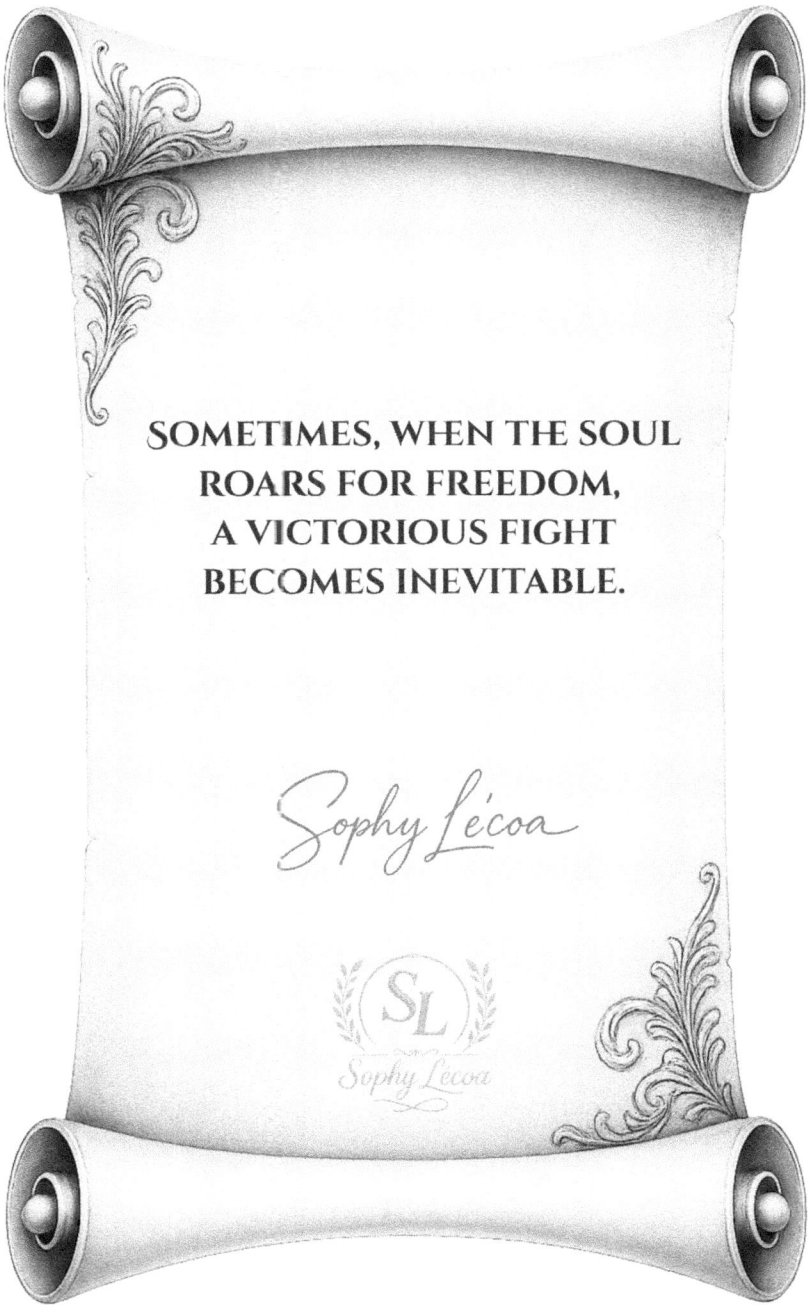

SOMETIMES, WHEN THE SOUL
ROARS FOR FREEDOM,
A VICTORIOUS FIGHT
BECOMES INEVITABLE.

Sophy Lécoa

Chapter 20

A "YES" to Myself

There are small moments in childhood that change
everything—
not with thunder,
but with a whisper brave enough to speak.

I still remember the first time I told Mama "No."

It wasn't born from rebellion.
It didn't come with stomping feet or a raised voice.
It came from a quieter place — deep inside —
where my longing to be seen finally met the courage to be
heard.

That day, Mama was in her usual rhythm — assigning
tasks the way she always did:
"After this, you can go out and play."

But every time we finished one thing, another followed.
"Just fold these."

"Now sweep that."

"Then carry this."

Clara, sweet and silent as ever,

obeyed without question —

graceful in her willingness, delicate in her quietness.

But something inside me… paused.

It started in my chest —

a knot, a tension, a quiet pull —

like a small, determined hand knocking from the inside, asking to be let out.

I stopped.

I looked up at Mama.

When I spoke, my voice was calm, but it carried something new —

a thread of boundary,

a breath of my own becoming.

"No, Mama… why don't you let me go play?"

She turned, surprise flickering in her eyes.

Her gaze searched my face — not in anger,

but as though she were seeing something unexpected take root.

"Because you still have more to do," she replied, steady but measured.

I hesitated. My hands curled into little fists at my sides. "But Mama… it'll be dark by the time I finish. I don't know when the tasks will end."

She stood still, looking at me in a way I had never felt before —

not like a child caught misbehaving,

but like someone watching a flower open for the first time.

Then — she smiled. Soft. Real.

A sound followed, rare and precious: she laughed.

Not mockingly, not dismissively,

but with a warmth that felt like a door opening.

"Alright," she said. "After this one, I'll let you go."

"Promise?" I asked, serious but steadier now.

"Promise."

I finished the last task with my heart already halfway outside.

But then — her voice again:

"Just one more, and then—"

I turned, *no longer afraid.*

"No, Mama. Please... you promised."

It wasn't a scream.

It wasn't a tantrum.

It was simply a truth — rooted now.

She froze.

And then — full, warm laughter spilled out.

"Alright, you can go now."

"Can Clara come too?"

She turned to my sister, who had been quietly folding a towel.

Clara's eyes flicked to mine — part worry, part wonder — as if she had just seen me grow a year older in a moment.

"Do you want to go with Sophy, Clara?"

"Yes, Mama."

Mama nodded, wrapping our scarves tighter.
The wool scratched our necks, but it felt like a hug she didn't
have time to give with her hands.

"Go. But listen to me — don't cross the street. Stay together. Look out for one another. Be polite. Be kind. Be back in
one hour."

And just like that, we stepped into the world —
into the wind —
into a small freedom that, for me, *felt like a revolution.*

It wasn't just about playing.
It was about being heard.
About learning that even a small voice could ripple through
the day and change it.

Clara didn't say a word, but I felt her walk closer to me.
She didn't take my hand — she didn't need to.

That evening, *I didn't feel just like a child anymore.*
I felt like someone *becoming.*
Not only obedient, but *aware.*
Not only a daughter, but *a voice.*

~ ~ ~ ~ ~ ✧ ~ ~ ~ ~ ~

What Life Whispered to Me

Sometimes, the biggest change comes from the small-
est sound.
It doesn't take a thunderstorm to shift a life.
Sometimes it takes only one whispered boundary.
One truth spoken aloud.
One small word in a big world.

No.

That day, I learned that power doesn't have to shout.
That love doesn't vanish when you speak your truth.
That a mother can smile when her daughter finds her
voice.

And sometimes, the first time you say "No"
is the first time you truly say "Yes" to yourself.

And that yes… echoes —
across years,
across choices,
across every breath of freedom that follows.

— Sophy Le'coa

~ ~ ~ ~ ~ ✧ ~ ~ ~ ~ ~

THAT DAY,
MY "NO" TO A CHORE
BECAME
THE FIRST "YES" TO MYSELF.

Sophy Lécoa

Chapter 21

The Flip-Flops and the Rising Stars

A new atmosphere had settled over our home—
not loud or stormy,
but a quiet, *constant pressure.*
We all felt it, yet no one named it.
Every step, every word, was measured to avoid upsetting Mama.
We tiptoed around emotions,
skipped the silly games we once played,
and even our conversations became clipped,
precisely pronounced—
a rule Mama herself had set.
That year, Clara and I performed at our absolute best in
school.
Mama was proud.
Her praise came sparingly, but when it did, it was gold.

Clara, as always, was the teacher's favorite—
composed, diligent, responsible.
I matched her achievements,
but for different reasons.

It wasn't love for the extra classes,
the tutors,
the exhaustion.
It was fear—
that if I slipped,
it would weigh on Mama's already fragile heart.

I was just over ten when summer vacation began—
and Mama gave us the most unexpected gift.

She had barely stepped through the door before Clara
and I dove into her brown leather purse like two starving
piglets.
"What did you get us?" I asked, already rummaging.
"Nothing. Not today," she said, stepping back.

"She got us something," I whispered to Clara.
"She always says that and then—"

But this time—no chocolate,
no gum,
not even a Lux soap.

Clara took the purse from me and searched with
surgical care.
Her fingers brushed against a folded envelope.
"Mama..." she said slowly, eyes widening,
"are these... tickets? To the beach?"

I snatched them, hardly daring to breathe.
"Is it true? Are we going?"

Mama's lips curved into a smile,
her eyes brightening like a match struck in the dark.
"Yes. Ten days. Ten nights. Just us three."
We screamed, hugging her so hard she almost lost her
balance.
It had been years since we'd gone to the seaside—
not since Daddy was alive.
I remembered the salty breeze,
the train ride,
the tiny fish I caught in my toy basket,
and Clara and I's shared bathtub in the hotel.
It had all felt like a dream.
And now we were going again—
only Mama this time,
but she was enough for two parents.

When the day came, Mama sat us at the table,
opened her wallet, and said:
"This is all we'll have to spend on this vacation."
Inside were the little labeled envelopes—
so familiar by row—
stacked in neat, flat piles.
"This one is for food—same amount each day.
This one's for entertainment—we'll go to a show or movie
every evening.
And this—" she lifted it like a prize—
"is EXTRA. For little things: gum, corn on the cob, cotton
candy… maybe a small souvenir."

My heart could have burst.
The EXTRA pile was the dream.

We traveled overnight.
Clara and I curled together and slept,
but Mama stayed awake the whole time—
our quiet sentinel.
Eight hours of rattling cars,
sticky heat,
and strangers' voices over the rustle of sandwich paper—
but none of it mattered.
At the end of it,
the Black Sea was waiting.
And the waves welcomed us like old friends.

In our tiny rental room, I unpacked my bag…
and froze.
No flip-flops. An idea came to mind:
"Mama," I said solemnly,
"I've decided I'll walk on my hands this vacation.
It's more fun."
She stared—then laughed.
But I didn't.
I flipped upside down and started walking,
palms smacking the path to the beach,
bare feet waving in the air.
People stared like we belonged to a circus.
Some smiled.
Some shook their heads.

"See, Mama? I don't need flip-flops!"

The next day, she returned with a yellow plastic pair.

Too big.

Not fancy.

Perfect, for my sore hands.

Clara, on the other hand, wore her shyness like armor.

She could throw fists at anyone who hurt me,

but ask for something she wanted?

Silence.

One afternoon, we wandered through a market near the shore.

Trinkets swayed in the salt air.

And then—Clara stopped.

Tiny white star earrings.

Delicate. Glowing.

"Do you like them?" Mama asked.

Clara nodded, barely breathing.

"Then go ask the lady what time it is," Mama said.

"If you do, the earrings are yours."

Clara froze.

I watched my warrior sister and saw her hesitate.

"I'll do it," I said.

Mama sighed.

"Sophy, will you stop being Clara's lawyer for once?"

But I couldn't.

I ran, asked, returned.

Clara got the earrings that day.

And my loyalty—louder than stars.

One evening, we walked back from the beach,
sugar still on our lips from cotton candy.

Earlier, we'd seen a stage show—
Mirabela Dauer singing one of her famous love songs.
I clapped the loudest.

That night, in the dark, I whispered:
"Do you think Mirabela's in love?"

Clara giggled.
"Maybe… but she sings like she's heartbroken."

The next day, she nudged me.
"Ask Mama if we can go on the water slide one more time."

"Why me?"
"She says yes to you more often."

So I asked.
Mama said yes.

We slid down together—
into the sun,
into the waves,
into something we didn't yet have words for.

That summer, *we began to understand Mama.*

The way she never took a bite of what she gave us.
How her "No, you eat it"
wasn't refusal—
it was protection.

From the little she had,
she wanted all of it to be ours.

That vacation became *a chapter made of light.*
We were mother and daughters.
We were grief and joy in the same breath.
We were flip-flops and rising stars.

And somewhere in that gentle, unspoken summer,
a small part of us began to heal.
A small part of us grew up.
And maybe—
a small part of her softened too.

~ ~ ~ ~ ~ ✧ ~ ~ ~ ~ ~

What Life Whispered to Me

Sometimes, the heaviest grief gives birth to the lightest joy—
a yellow pair of flip-flops,
a laugh from Mama,
cotton candy spun like a dream and stuck sweetly to our cheeks.

I learned that healing doesn't always arrive in grand gestures.
Sometimes, it's ten days on the beach with the people you love.
It's saying, I'll walk on my hands if I have to.
It's noticing the earrings your sister is too shy to ask for
and offering your voice instead.

Life taught me that joy is not the absence of pain—
but the courage to keep playing while carrying it.
To smile while your hands sting.
To laugh even as the waves pull away.

Because somehow,
the most fragile summers
are the ones that last forever.

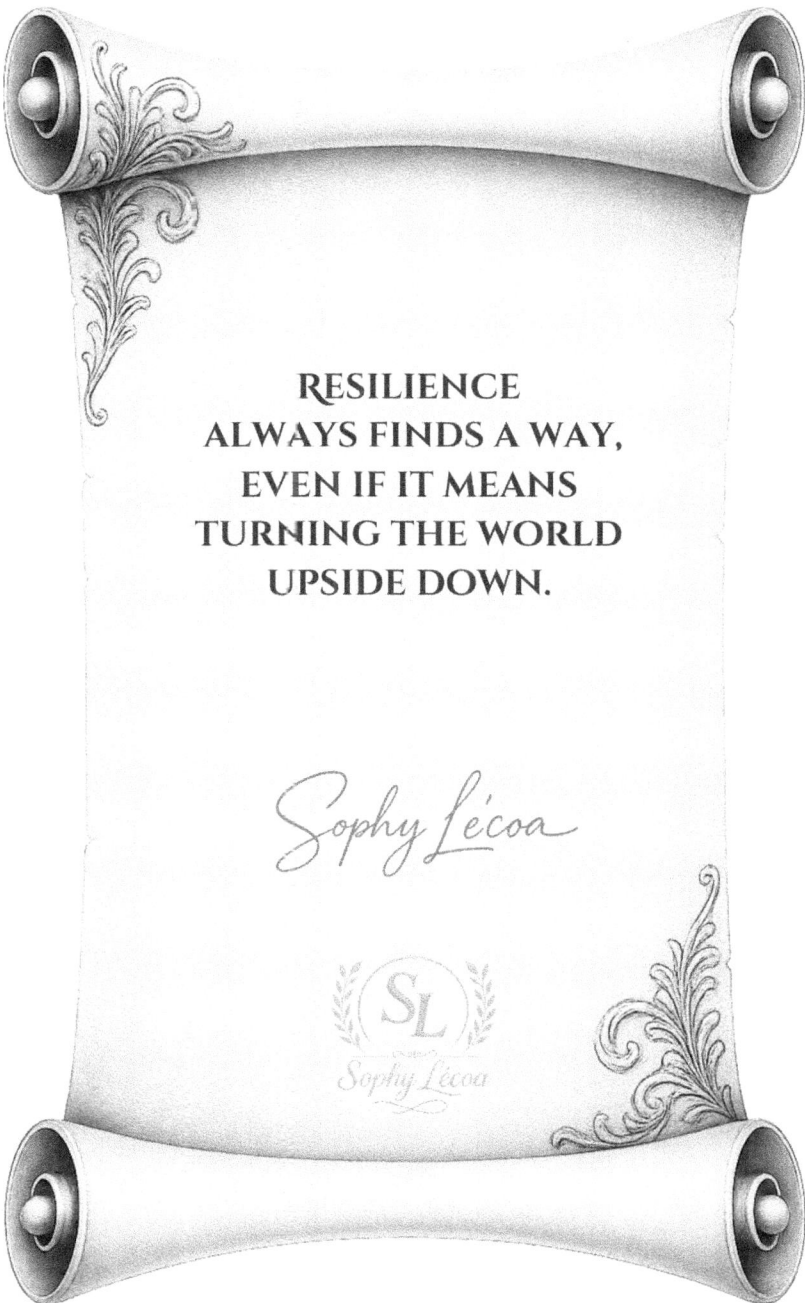

**RESILIENCE
ALWAYS FINDS A WAY,
EVEN IF IT MEANS
TURNING THE WORLD
UPSIDE DOWN.**

Sophy Lécoa

Chapter 22

Mama: The Silent Backbone

She never raised her voice,
but the world listened.

Not because she was loud,
but because she was steady.

She didn't just hold us together—
she was the frame that kept us standing.
The invisible glue.
The quiet force that kept everything in place.

Mama never remarried.
She never dated—at least, not that I ever saw.
Her life revolved around two things:
us… and duty.

She kept guests away—not from coldness, but from
conviction.
Quiet meant focus, and focus meant success.

Sometimes she even unplugged the phone,
just to make sure nothing disturbed the peace.

Our house was not a social place.
It was a sanctuary for learning.

We weren't allowed to visit others much either.
After the nail polish incident with Aunt Vio,
I stopped altogether.

Birthday parties?
Two, maybe three in total—
and only if Mama could find a simple present,
which wasn't often.

She sheltered us.
But more than that—she trained us.

Every detail mattered.
Grammar. Posture. Manners.

She knitted everything herself—
socks, gloves, sweaters, dresses, even winter coats.
Some yarn was so thick we joked it could stop a bullet—
and in winter, it almost felt like it could.

Even our tights were handmade—
delicate, white, with lace-like patterns
that left imprints on our skin after hours at school.
But they were beautiful.
And people noticed.

Not just our clothes—
but how clean we looked.
How prepared.
How… different.

Mama didn't drink coffee.
She didn't smoke.
She didn't gossip.
She had no debt,
no dramatic love life,
no time to waste.
What she had, she wielded with precision.
When the kitchen sink broke,
she hired a plumber.
I remember how she stood behind him,
arms crossed, watching everything.
Too close. Too curious.
A little too much.
He looked annoyed.
Mama didn't care.
She was learning.
The next time the sink broke,
she fixed it herself—without a moment's hesitation.
Stove? Fixed.
Leaky pipe? Fixed.
Loose door hinge? Tightened.
She even kept a small notebook—
patterns, measurements, repairs, diets.
Not because she enjoyed it,
but *because she needed to*.
We depended on her knowing everything.
So she did.
For my gymnastics diet,
she calculated vitamins and calories

on tiny paper scraps pinned to the fridge.

Meals were cooked fresh at 4 a.m.,

portioned exactly,

designed to fuel me.

They weren't pretty,

but they gave me the strength to keep performing.

And when life threw little storms at us,

Mama handled them with the same quiet precision.

At the playground, when drama broke out,

it was often because Clara—my fierce protector—

had stepped in to shield me from the rougher kids.

She didn't hesitate,

and her way of defending me sometimes landed us in trouble.

Mama always went in person to speak with the other parents.

Not to argue.

Not to accuse.

But to smooth the blow.

She offered help.

Told them—with a smile that never wavered—

that if they ever needed medical treatment,

day or night, they could count on her.

And though she'd tell them we would be punished,

we never were.

Once home, she would simply say:

"Look after each other... but be kinder. Leave the drama."

She knew every child had a father to protect them from bullies.

She also knew Clara was mine.

At the hospital, she treated patients
day and night.
Colleagues used to say,
"Rozi's the one you want on call at midnight."
Because she always showed up.

At home, she never hit us—not once.
She didn't need to.
She spoke with her eyes.

If I had to write a book about *her glances,*
it would have chapters

The You Better Stop Look
The I Love You But You're Pushing It Look
The I See Through You Look

Her hair was always neat—
either twisted into a ballerina bun
or falling in soft curls.

Her nails were short and clean.
Makeup? Just a line of kohl at her eyes
and a touch of gloss.

And the scent of Freesia—
cheap communist perfume—
was her signature.

Even now, when I smell that flower,
it feels like home.

When Mama gave her word,
she kept it.
Never late.
Never empty promises.

Her punctuality was like a Swiss clock.
Her respect for authority was unshakable—
and, in turn, it earned her theirs.

From the commander of the hospital
to the last soldier in the line—
all greeted her with admiration.

Before they called her *The Cat With Seven Lives*,
they called her *Margaret Thatcher*.

Not out of mockery—
but respect.

She was precise. Correct. Fast. Stoic.
Focused.
And never distracted by gossip or games.

She never asked to be seen—
yet everything in our lives stood because of her.

~ ~ ~ ~ ~ ✧ ~ ~ ~ ~ ~

What Life Whispered to Me

There are people we admire so much,
they almost stop feeling human.

Their strength becomes legend.
Their presence — unshakable.

For me, that person was Mama.

Even as a child,
I looked up to her with awe.
Grateful.
Proud.
Inspired.
But also... distant.

So many of her qualities felt carved from stone —
discipline, precision, silence, sacrifice.

I adopted many of them.
Not because I was told to,
but because I saw how powerful they were.
They worked.

But with time, I learned something else:
that strength doesn't always mean control.
That love doesn't always mean sacrifice.

That you can honor what built you...
and still choose softer ways to live.

And maybe, just maybe,
the greatest tribute to a silent backbone —
is a voice that can finally say:

I see you.
I thank you.
And I now choose my own way to walk forward.

— Sophy Le'coa

~ ~ ~ ~ ~ ✧ ~ ~ ~ ~ ~ ~

SOME PEOPLE
DON'T ASK TO BE SEEN —
YET EVERYTHING STANDS
BECAUSE OF THEM.

Sophy Lécoa

Chapter 23

The Voices from Beyond

Mama's presence lingered
even when she wasn't there.
Her silence.
Her discipline.
Her quiet, unshakable strength.
They stayed in the air,
like the scent of freshly ironed laundry
or the crisp folds of neatly stacked sheets.
They shaped the way we moved.
The way we spoke.
The way we didn't speak.
But there were moments
when the walls seemed to loosen,
when the air felt different—
like something hidden was waiting to be found.

It began on a day like that—
calm on the surface,
but humming with a secret underneath.

Clara leaned in close,
her voice barely louder than a breath,
her eyes gleaming—
serious and excited at the same time.

"They say if you tie a long wire to the back of the radio
and stretch it out like an antenna…
you can catch something different."

That word—*different*—tasted like a spell.

And just like that,
we were no longer two little girls
trapped between schoolbooks and silences.

We were scientists.
Explorers.
Revolutionaries in disguise.

Clara rummaged through the toolbox
and pulled out an old copper wire,
slightly bent at the ends.

We stretched it along the wall,
from bookshelf to curtain rod,
careful not to make a sound that would raise suspicion.

Then—
with both reverence and mischief—
we connected it to the back of the radio.

The dial was big,
smooth,
and full of possibility.

I took a breath and turned it slowly.

Static.

Buzz.

Crackle.

And then... a voice.

"This... is the Voice of America."

We froze.

Our eyes widened like lanterns in the dark.

Then we smiled.

It was real.

Through all the dust and static,
something was breaking through—
something forbidden.

The signal faded in and out,
like a whisper from another world.

We scrambled for chairs,
lifting the wire higher,
holding it aloft like a sacred thread.

One of us would hold it up—
arms stretched, legs wobbling—
while the other adjusted the dial,
chasing fleeting fragments of clarity.

It wasn't just noise.

It was light.

It was truth.

There were no Party songs.

No hollow slogans.

No manufactured joy.

Instead, voices spoke freely —
calm and steady —
about the world,
about freedom,
about justice.

Some belonged to Romanians —
political defectors who had escaped to America.
I had heard murmurs about them for years —
how only a few ever made it,
and how terrible the punishment was
for those caught trying.

And yet here they were...
speaking in our own language,
their voices crossing oceans,
telling stories without fear,
as if no border or wall could silence them.

I felt a fierce pride for them.
They had made it —
to America,
to freedom.

"How courageous they must be," I whispered,
"to speak so openly."

Clara nodded.
"They're not rushing.
They're not hiding."

"That's because they're somewhere
they don't have to," I said.

Every word felt like it had been waiting for us—
like it was giving voice
to the thoughts we had been taught to bury.

It was as if someone, far away,
had reached into our silence
and spoken aloud the things
we didn't even dare to think.

We learned that some people stood up.
That communism wasn't praised everywhere—
it was questioned.
That dictators could fall.
That truth could be broadcast boldly,
even across oceans.

In that moment,
we weren't just children in a cold apartment.
We were part of something bigger.
We were waking up.

Every time Mama was at work,
we were at the radio.

Lights off.
Curtains drawn.
Hearts pounding with a mixture of guilt and defiance.

The room was dim and still…
but inside us,
a fire was catching—
a fire we couldn't name yet,
but could never put out.

We weren't supposed to hear it.
But the soul doesn't ask for permission.

Those forbidden voices—
scratchy, fading, almost too faint to catch—
were more powerful than anything we had ever known.

They told us *the truth was alive.*
And that we were not alone.

We started *seeing everything differently.*
At school.
At our teachers' words.
At the parades.
At the red flags.
At *Ceaușescu's* face
watching from every wall.

Because now we knew something
that could never be unlearned:

There is more.

More than they showed us.
More than they allowed us to believe.

We lived in *two worlds.*
One gray and *scripted.*
The other *invisible—but real.*

One forced into obedience.
The other calling to us
like a far-off melody.

And every time we turned that dial
and caught a glimpse of that faraway voice,
our hope grew bolder.

Because deep inside,
we no longer wondered
if things would ever change.

We knew.
It was just a matter of when.
And in that stillness,
in that secret room,
we heard the future calling.

~ ~ ~ ~ ~ ✧ ~ ~ ~ ~ ~

What Life Whispered to Me

Sometimes,
living inside a lie so big,
the mind forgets it's a lie.
But the soul never forgets.

When it hears the truth,
it recognizes.
It remembers.

Fear can dress itself as truth.
Obedience can masquerade as peace.
But deep down,
the soul knows.

Even without proof,
something in you whispers:
There's more.

More than you're told.
More than you're allowed to imagine.

The first time I heard the Voice of America,
it wasn't just static and sound.
It was like a part of me—

long buried —
stood up and took a breath.

Truth doesn't beg for attention.
It simply rings in your chest
like a bell.

From that day forward,
what I was told
was never enough anymore.

I needed to see.
To question.
To know for myself.

Because real truth
doesn't try to convince you.
It reminds you
who you've been all along.

-— Sophy Le'coa

~ ~ ~ ~ ~ ✧ ~ ~ ~ ~ ~

WHEN TRUTH IS MET,
DOESN'T TRY TO CONVINCE —
IT CALLS YOU BACK
TO WHO
YOU REALLY ARE.

Sophy Lécoa

Chapter 24

The Danger in the Sound

The first time we heard it, we thought we could keep it
forever.
The Voice of America—our *secret window to a bigger world.*
The fire that lit up our quiet apartment.
We couldn't wait to be alone.
It was becoming our forbidden routine.
We were always careful.
Curtains drawn.
Lights off.
Wire tucked neatly away before Mama came home.
But danger doesn't always knock.
And even in our excitement, a thin thread of unease
sometimes trailed behind the sound—
like a shadow following the voice through the static,
reminding us that nothing this bright could stay hidden
forever.

It happened one late afternoon.
The air was heavy —
the kind of stillness that made the radio's hiss seem louder.

The afternoons had taken on a strange electricity.
The curiosity that once made us eavesdrop on our neighbors'
music had vanished;
now all we craved was that single, hushed moment of solitude
when we could tune in again, learn more, discover more.

With every word we caught through the static,
I felt as if I'd known it all along.
The truth didn't feel new —
it felt remembered,
like meeting an old friend I hadn't seen since birth.

The apartment was so still,
yet the faint sounds from next door — music, voices, laughter —
seemed impossibly loud,
as if the whole world were unaware of the treasure we held in
our hands.

We listened so intently that everything else dissolved.
Every creak, every murmur, every distant noise melted away,
until it felt as though we were floating in a dream
where sound no longer existed —
except for that one forbidden voice from beyond,
slipping through the static to whisper only to us.

Sometimes my eyes wandered to Daddy's chair.
I wondered if he could have been one of those Romanian
heroes helping from abroad.
But then — what would that have meant for us?

Did this man have a family?

Were they with him in America?

Were they punished, left behind... or gone forever?

The questions chilled me,

but I wanted the answers.

I leaned closer to the radio,

hoping that somewhere between the words, I might find them.

And then—

without warning—

Mama appeared in the doorway.

In one sharp motion, she switched off the radio.

Silence.

I didn't startle.

It felt as though my body froze between two worlds—

the living room in front of me,

and the shimmering, untouchable land of voices

that had just been torn away.

Her eyes fell on the radio.

On us.

On the copper wire snaking across the floor.

Her voice was low. Too low.

„De unde ați învățat să faceți asta?"

("Where did you learn to do this?")

Clara glanced at me, her lips pressed into a thin,

nervous line.

Mama didn't wait for an answer.

She crossed the room in quick strides,

pulled the wire free with one swift motion,

and set it aside.

Her face was pale,
but her voice… steady.

„Știți ce s-ar putea întâmpla dacă cineva v-ar auzi as-
cultând asta?"
("Do you know what could happen if someone heard you
listening to that?")

We didn't.
Not fully.

And then she told us.

Not every detail—
but enough to freeze the air in our lungs.

Arrests.
Interrogations.
Families destroyed over a rumor, a whisper,
a song from the wrong station.

She spoke quietly,
but the fear in her voice
was louder than anything the radio had ever played.

We promised we wouldn't do it again.
We meant it.
At least for a while.

Once she left the room,
we both looked down for a long time.
Clara reached for my hand and gave it a squeeze.

I could hear my heartbeat—
fast but muffled—
with a *strange mixture of panic and sorrow.*

The silence that followed was no longer the kind that
protected us;

it was the kind that pressed against your chest,
making each breath feel measured and heavy.

But the thing about truth is—
once you've heard it,
silence feels like a cage.

And cages, no matter how safe they seem,
were never meant to be permanent.

~ ~ ~ ~ ~ ✧ ~ ~ ~ ~ ~

What Life Whispered to Me

Sometimes fear doesn't shout—
it squeezes your breath,
tightens your chest,
wraps icy hands around your voice.

It makes you freeze.
Hide.
Obey.

But even in fear, life gives you a choice:
Withdraw… or listen again.

Mama wasn't wrong.
It was dangerous.
It was real.

And we still did it again—
not because we forgot the risk,
but because something in us knew:

The truth is worth hearing.

Even in secret.
Even in darkness.
Even through the hum of a trembling radio.

Life whispered to me then:
True courage isn't the absence of fear —
it's the force that keeps you going,
even when your heart is trembling.

— Sophy Le'coa

~ ~ ~ ~ ~ ✧ ~ ~ ~ ~ ~

TRUE COURAGE
IS THE FORCE
THAT KEEPS YOU GOING,
EVEN WITH
A TREMBLING HEART.

Sophy Lécoa

Chapter 25

Strings in the Dark

The summer of 1987 was a balancing act—
between the world I knew
and the one I was beginning to imagine.
Clara had just finished tenth grade,
a full-on high school girl with new friends,
bigger laughter,
and long walks that didn't always include me.
She was still my sister, still my fierce protector—
but sometimes her world no longer had space for mine.
So, on many afternoons,
I found myself alone, leaning close to the radio.
That summer, my treasures were small
but rich with meaning:
a few stamps in my cloşar (stamp album),
most of them won in playful bets

or gifted by neighborhood kids who simply liked me.
And a growing pile of foreign candy and chewing gum
wrappers—
each one traded for something better.

The best trade I ever made
was ten wrappers for a glossy Tina Turner sticker.
I didn't just keep it—
I pressed it onto my new guitar.
In that moment, I felt impossibly sophisticated,
as if a piece of the forbidden outside world
had slipped past the borders
and found its way into my hands.

Mama had brought home that guitar just a week
earlier.
I don't know if it was to distract me
from talking about dangerous things—like America—
or simply because she had seen how much I wanted one.
It didn't matter.
It was mine.
And now it carried Tina Turner's face.

The lessons began.
Soon the radio wasn't my only companion.

One evening, under the weak glow of a candle,
my fingers moved from note to note without hesitation—
no pauses, no mistakes.
Clara sat nearby, listening.
Mama was folding laundry.
Then she stopped, smiled, and clapped.

It was the kind of applause
that wraps itself around your heart
and stays there.

I learned my first real song—
My Bonnie Lies Over the Ocean.
It was American,
and I sang it softly in English,
saying aloud the kinds of things
I could never say in Romanian.

Soon Clara learned to play too.
We became a duo—
two voices, one guitar,
the Tina Turner sticker gleaming faintly on its body.
We were mesmerizing to everyone—
but most of all, to ourselves.
It felt like my best friend had come back to me.

That same summer, Mama hired tutors to keep us
studying.
I decided early on that if I could steer my physics tutor
into talking about things I liked,
the lesson would pass faster.

One day, I pushed it too far—
I hadn't done my homework.

"Why didn't you do your assignment?"
"Because I was busy with something very important."
"And what was that?"
"I wrote a song on my guitar."
"And that was important to you?"

"Yes. Creativity expands the brain.
And a bigger brain has more space to absorb... physics, for
example."

He laughed but shook his head.
"I'm afraid I'll have to tell your mother."

"No, please! Let me play it for you—you'll love it!"

"Haha... I'm sure it's a good song,
but we need to start now.
Your mother is paying good money for this session,
and you're wasting it."

"Alright," I sighed. "But I have a question."

"Nothing new there. What is it this time?"

"When do doctors ever use all these formulas and
physics problems?"

"Well... they don't. But you need to know them to get
into medical school."

"So I have to stuff them into my brain
just to have something to forget later?"

"Physics knowledge applies to many other important
fields.
Like scientific research, for example."

"But why does everyone have to learn something
that only a researcher will actually use?
That's not fair."

"Life's not fair," he sighed.

"I think we can make it fair.
We just all have to want it."

"Yes... maybe in heaven."

"Maybe we are in heaven.
We just have to heal it." I said.
        He studied me for a moment, then smiled.
"You know, you're an expert at dragging things out."
        We continued the session,
but my thoughts kept slipping away—
back to my new guitar,
back to my new song—
drifting into a dream world
filled with beautiful, exciting things
no formula could ever measure.

~ ~ ~ ~ ~ ✧ ~ ~ ~ ~ ~

What Life Whispered to Me

Some treasures are made of paper and glue.
Others of string and wood.

But the rarest treasures are not things at all—
they are the moments when something, or someone,
finds their way back to you.

Dreams do not die when silenced;
they learn to hide in plain sight.

Sometimes they wait quietly—
in a song, in a sticker,
in the faint glow of candlelight—
until the day they are ready
to sing again.

— Sophy Le'coa

~ ~ ~ ~ ~ ✧ ~ ~ ~ ~ ~

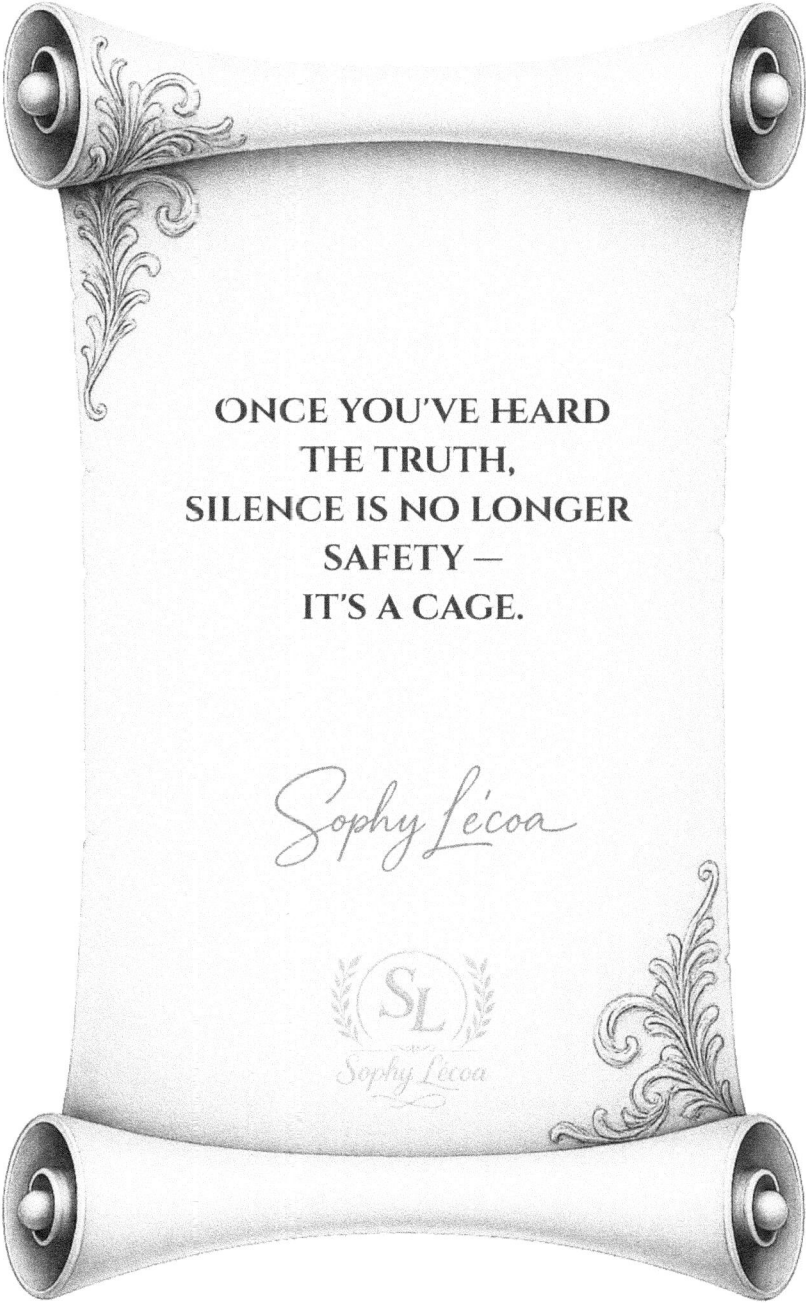

ONCE YOU'VE HEARD
THE TRUTH,
SILENCE IS NO LONGER
SAFETY —
IT'S A CAGE.

Sophy Lécoa

Chapter 26

Some Doctor with Carpenter Hands

When September 15th arrived and school began again,
6th grade finally brought physics—
something I had already studied ahead of time over the
summer.
It was boring class.
I had new passions now,
but the old ones stayed too.
With the tools Mama always used to give us
everything,
I tried to do the same—
except I used them like someone with two left hands.
I fumbled.
I forced.
I made messes more often than not…
but I was determined to create something of my own.

The colored threads meant for hems and socks,
I used to give Luiza new hair.
I made clothes from leftover scraps of Mama's sewing.
I fixed broken toys with a hammer,
always stopping just a little too late.

Always crafting.
Always building.
Always attempting.
Just like Mama.

Monkey see, monkey do.
And then there was the more—
the secret inventions and quiet experiments
I did without Mama's knowledge.
Always at the wrong time,
but shown to her at the right moment,
when it was too late to scold me.

I'd present them with a proud grin,
and she'd either smile, shake her head,
or—most often—sigh deeply and say:
"Please… can you stop already?"

But I couldn't.
Because her tools had become mine.
And even if my stitches were crooked
and my hammer too loud,
the desire to create—
to fix, to build, to make something last—
was already alive inside me.

At school, physics brought new things:
lab notebooks, formulas… and white coats.

One afternoon, Mama brought me a real one from the
hospital.
Not a costume—
a proper, crisp, adult-sized lab coat.

I wore it around the house like a crown.
I felt grown.
Important.
Chosen.

Then one day, while switching labs with another class,
I saw her.
The top student in the school.
She stood at the front like a sculpture—
calm, brilliant, untouchable.

And she wore *the most beautiful lab coat* I had ever seen.
Not stiff or yellowing like the others,
but white—pure, elegant,
flowing like a dress from the collar down.
Buttoned in the back.
Initials stitched in purple thread.

It looked less like a uniform
and more like something from another world.
It looked American to me.
And suddenly, I needed one just like it.

At home, I remembered something:
a white sheet from Morocco.
A gift to Mama.
Still sealed in plastic.

Reserved, she once said, for a special guest—
maybe a queen.
Folded.
Waiting.
Sacred.

That Sunday, I told Mama my head hurt.
She and Clara went out without me.
And I... I got to work.

I opened the sealed package like treasure.
Laid the sheet across the living room carpet.
And—holding my breath—
cut right through the center.

Then I pulled out Mama's sewing machine.
The thread tangled.
The fabric slipped.
The sleeves turned out tight.
The hem was uneven.

But I finished.
Just in time.
I heard keys in the door,
shoes shuffling,
Mama's voice calling my name.

I shoved the machine away, swept scraps aside,
and stood up, heart pounding.

"Are you feeling better?" Mama asked gently.
"Yes," I said—too quickly.
She started toward the kitchen—
then stopped.

Near the couch lay a scrap of white fabric,
betraying everything.

Her eyes widened.

"Sophy... what did you do?"

Clara froze in the hallway,
eyes bouncing between us.

"I saved you money, Mama," I whispered.

She stared at me.

And then—she laughed.

Not polite.

Not scolding.

But the kind that bursts out when your heart gives up
and gives in all at once.

Big. Honest. Uncontrolled.

"Oh, Sophy," she said, wiping a tear.

"Let me see what you've done this time."

So I showed her.

The coat was stiff.

The sleeves tight.

The seams uneven.

But to me, it was a masterpiece.

She ran her fingers over the fabric.

"You will wear this even when you become a doctor,"
she said finally, still smiling.

"I'm not buying you another one until then."

I grinned.

"Thank you, Mama."

Later, Clara confessed in a whisper:
"I wore it too."
"You did?" I gasped.
She nodded, half-laughing.
"It was too small. Twisted in the back.
I couldn't even move my arms. But I didn't care."
Neither of us did.
That coat—uneven, stubborn,
stitched from something sacred—
had *become a symbol* of something more:
Possibility.
Play.
Creation.
Daring.
Mama never said so, but I think she understood.
Even if it took her two full days
to fix and tune the sewing machine I had "borrowed."
She didn't yell.
She just sighed, wiped the grease from her hands.
"Doamna doctor... da' cu mâini de tâmplar."
("Some doctor... with the hands of a carpenter.")
And before walking away, she added quietly:
"Next time, tell me before you turn my house into a design
studio."
I didn't promise.
Because there would be a next time.
And deep down... she knew it too.

What Life Whispered to Me

Some things can be replaced.
But a child's joy—
that's one-of-a-kind.

That's what Mama knew.

She never said it out loud,
but I've come to understand:
She valued us more than the rarest items in the house.

Even when it meant sacrificing something beautiful,
imported,
or impossible to replace—

A Moroccan sheet.
A sewing machine.
Her time.
Her peace.
Her patience.

All offered silently, lovingly—
for our growth,
our delight,
our mistakes turned into meaning.

I now see what I couldn't then:
things are here to serve us —
not the other way around.

And Mama never served things.
She served love.

And somehow,
through crooked stitches and brave little hands,
I began to do the same.

— Sophy Le'coa

~ ~ ~ ~ ~ ✧ ~ ~ ~ ~ ~

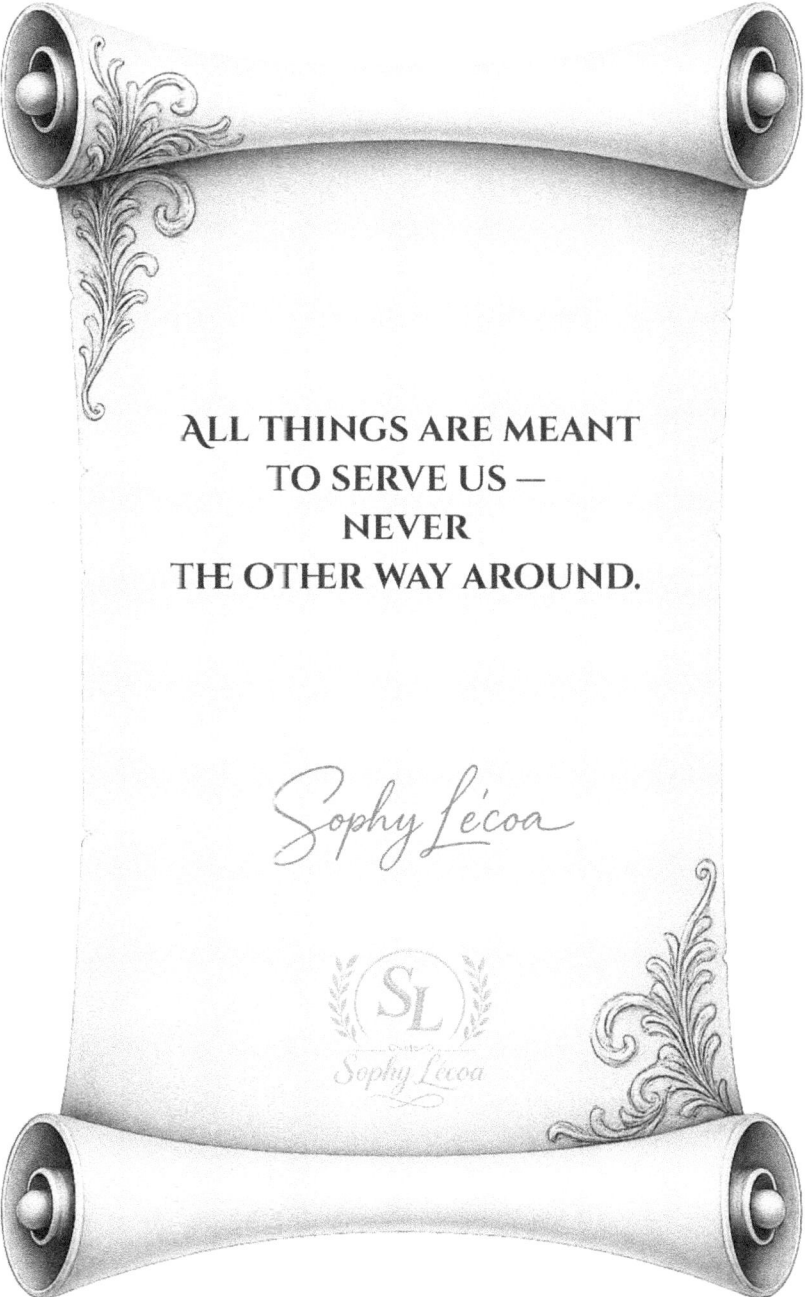

ALL THINGS ARE MEANT
TO SERVE US —
NEVER
THE OTHER WAY AROUND.

Sophy Lécoa

Chapter 27

Not Going Back

By the end of September 1987, the pull of the radio was
too strong to ignore.
I found myself sneaking back to it,
even as Mama doubled down on my studies.
She brought home the toughest math teacher she could
find —
a man who taught formulas as if they were alive.
My days became a balance of notes and numbers,
music and mathematics.
Still, the radio waited.
And no matter how bright the candlelight was,
its signal called through the dark.

That winter, whispers ran through *Brașov.*
The city buzzed with news of rebellion at the big factory.
Tens of thousands of workers had taken to the streets —

chanting, defying the regime.

And then it was over.

Crushed before the world could see.

My heart ached, but I hoped it wasn't the end.

I listened to the Voice of America more often now,

alone in the apartment—

Mama at work, Clara at school.

The more I listened,

the more I hated the life we were forced to live:

the slogans, the shortages,

the way joy was rationed like sugar and oil.

Meanwhile, Mama had her own war plan for me:

relentless tutoring to prepare for the most competitive high

school in the city.

Geometry, Algebra, Trigonometry, Literature and Grammer—

concepts for older students drilled into me in 6th and 7th

grade.

"So we can fix it all in 8th," she said.

"Then you'll be ready."

The competition was brutal:

80 kids for every single seat at *Pedagogic* High School.

Mama's dream was medical school,

but I bargained for *Pedagogic* instead—

hoping to escape medicine without open rebellion.

Four years.

Four years of childhood carved into notebooks and late nights,

of tutors and timed drills,

of Mama's dream pressed like an iron against my back.

In our city, the high school exam wasn't just a test.
It was a gate.
One of two great gates of a life—
the other came later, at university—
and both were fierce.
We were trained like athletes:
handwriting sharp as calligraphy,
grammar that clicked like gears,
math rehearsed until it became muscle memory.
Thirty seats at Pedagogic.
Hundreds of us pushing toward the same narrow door.
I was ready.

Day One — Romanian.
Three hours.
I wrote steady and elegant,
ink gliding, grammar shining,
literature nearly perfect.
I left the room light on my feet,
already hearing the whisper:
You did it.

Day Two — Mathematics.
A long wooden desk.
Sun pressing through high windows.
The quiet thunder of a hundred pens.
On my table:
one fountain pen filled with ink,
one pencil, one eraser, one scratch sheet.

Nothing more.

Nothing less.

The invigilator slit the sealed envelope,
placed the papers down one by one.
"You have three hours," she said.
"Begin."

I scanned the problems.
All my old friends were there—
angles I could see before drawing them,
equations that solved themselves when I breathed.
I started to write.

Twenty minutes in—
a tight pressure curled low in my stomach.
I ignored it. Kept going.

Thirty minutes in—
it sharpened.
My letters swelled.
A single blue teardrop of ink broke in the margin—
a tenth of point gone.

Forty minutes in—
I wasn't doing math anymore.
I was negotiating with my own body.
Two thoughts fought for space:
Solve.
Hold it.

Fifty minutes in—
the room tilted.

And the rule—our unspoken law—
flashed in my mind with brutal clarity:

Once you left during the exam,
you did not come back.

Not for any reason.

That was why every teacher had said:
Go now. Go before. Never during.

Two pages done. Three to go.
I could still make a 9.90.
If I stayed.
If I gambled.
If I let the worst happen and lived with the nickname forever.

Or—
I could stand up,
turn the handle,
and erase four years in a single click of the door.

My breath came shallow.
The nib scratched louder than the clock.
Another blot of ink bled into the paper like a bruise.

I stood.
Chair legs scraped.
Heads lifted.

I walked, eyes fixed on the wood grain of the door,
the brass handle,
the squeak as it turned.

I stepped through.

And that was it.
The rule sealed behind me like a vault.

I passed the bathroom.
Passed the corridor's echo.
Past the guard's chair.
Through the iron gate.
Into the heat.

And I ran.

Down the block, across the street,
lungs burning, legs hot with fury and shame,
the world streaking at the edges.
I ran all the way home.

The apartment was empty.
I closed the door and folded in on myself on the couch,
sobbing the kind of sobs that steal breath and give nothing
back.

Four years —
gone in twenty minutes and one door.

News carried faster than sound.
Mama's face when I told her —
shock first, then silence heavier than any shouting.
Tutors blinking as if they'd misheard.
Clara not knowing where to look.
Neighbors whispering in stairwells.
Friends in the courtyard,
everyone who had watched me train like the surest bet in
town.

And me —
the girl who left.

The school would not bend.
Mama went anyway, begged them for an oral exam—
anything, everything, the whole four years of math at once.
The answer was no.

That summer was a long hallway with no doors.
I stayed inside most days,
walked fast and aimless in the evenings when the air cooled.
Embarrassment sat like a stone in my throat.
Anxiety curled under my ribs.
Even the air felt rationed.
Toward the end of summer, I offered Mama a bridge.
"I'll study hard in high school," I told her.
"Physics, chemistry, anatomy—by heart. I'll get into Medical
School."
I didn't want that life, not truly.
But I wanted her shoulders to lower.
I wanted the house to breathe again.
She believed me.
She needed to.
But silently I prayed, someday, somehow, other planes might
come along.

Underneath, another drum kept beating.
The country was tightening.
Whispers traveled like contraband.
We had already lived through *Brașov's* workers—
tens of thousands brave enough to rise,
then vanish back into the machinery of fear.

I listened when I could.

I hated the greyness with a heat that frightened me.

I wanted the wall to crack.

I wanted air.

What Life Whispered to Me

Sometimes the air runs out long before the surface appears.
You kick harder, panic blooms,
and the water feels endless.

That summer, my dreams sank like stones—
heavy, sudden, impossible to lift.
Four years of sacrifice vanished in a few unbearable moments.
I was left grabbing for anything that might keep me afloat.

That's when the smile came.
Not the kind born of joy—
but the kind you carve
so the world won't see the cracks.

It became my quiet oxygen.
A breath I could carry anywhere.
A way to say I'm fine when I wasn't.

I didn't know it then,
but that smile would become my strongest weapon:
to calm others,

to protect myself,
to open doors silence would have kept shut.

I used to believe a single exam could define my life.
Now I know a closed door isn't the end of the house.
Sometimes it's the hallway
that leads you away from a room you were never
meant to live in.

Maybe that day —
walking out —
wasn't only a loss.

Maybe it was the first small refusal.
The first quiet act of choosing myself.
So soft no one heard it but me.

And sometimes,
the smallest act of leaving
is the first breath of the life you were meant to enter.

I carried the shame of that day like a brand.
But I also carried proof
that I would not live bound to rules that stole my
breath.

The loss was sharp,
but it shaped the muscle I would need for a larger
fight.
A fight that was coming for all of us.

Life whispered that not every ending is failure.
Some endings are the quiet rehearsal for courage.

WHEN MINUTES ERASE
YEARS OF EFFORT
AND LOSS FEELS HEAVY,
SOMETHING UNBREAKABLE
BEGINS TO FORM.

Sophy Lécoa

Chapter 28

The Waiting Grew Loud

When autumn came,
I stepped into ninth grade at a school I'd never dreamed of,
surrounded by kids who had played while I studied—
happy, loud, untouched by the weight I carried.
I loved them for their lightness.
I resented it, too.
It felt like I had traded four years of childhood
for a seat I didn't want.

The room we all lived in—
the country, the future, the tight-lipped house—
was running out of oxygen.

By day, the streets betrayed nothing.
Life marched on in gray routine—
workers flooding into factories,
queues coiling outside shops with empty shelves,
children bent under satchels.

It seemed as though nothing would ever happen,
as if the whole city had been embalmed in silence.
    And yet, when I tuned the hidden antenna,
another world opened.
From the crackle of the Voice of America
came news of protests, uprisings,
rumors of a system beginning to crack.
Their words burned with urgency and hope,
but around me everything remained a fluid grave.
Silent. Heavy. Unmoving.
    I often wondered if I was going mad—
living between two worlds:
one brimming with possibility,
the other suffocating under fear.
We had no power most nights;
I listened in the daytime when I could,
curtains drawn, ear pressed close,
my pulse louder than the broadcast.
    Fear, held long enough, *changes shape.*
The trembling gave way to a restless heat.
I could no longer bear another morning
under *Ceaușescu's* portrait,
another chorus of hollow slogans.
Even small joys turned to dust.
Jokes in the yard felt like borrowed air,
momentary distractions before the ache returned.
    Clara finished twelfth grade by then—
tall, quick-witted,
somehow both grounded and restless.

Mama had lined up mentors for me:
chemistry, physics, biology, Romanian, math.
"Excel at these," she said. "The rest—pass if you must."
And so I performed,
always out of fear of disappointing her.
Except for technical class.
In my head I called it the loser class.
I decided I would rather drive a tractor
through endless potato fields
than open those manuals.
Twos and threes bled down the register.
The threat of repeating ninth grade
grew heavier with each week—
the kind of shame no communist parent could bear.
I was so lost in my own contempt—
hating everything,
hating everyone—
that I never once stopped to look at myself.

Then came the day.
A cold afternoon.
That dreaded class.
I sat in the back, no notebook, no pen,
staring out the window,
already halfway gone.
A knock.
The door opened.
Mama stepped in.
My heart dropped into my shoes.

She spoke with the teacher in a low, steady voice
while the class sat frozen.
Then she turned.

"Sophy. In front."

I walked the aisle between rows of kids
I'd labeled "losers."
And then—without warning—
her hand.

A slap.

The sound cracked the room in two.
The sting bloomed across my cheek,
but the sharper strike landed deeper—
on my pride, my contempt, my illusions.

In that instant the world rearranged itself.
First: no one in that room was a bigger loser than me.
I was one of them.
Second: if I kept drifting,
I wouldn't just fail a class.
I would fail myself.

I went back to my seat in silence—
the kind of silence that rearranges a life.
The room looked different.
So did the faces.
So did I.

Meanwhile, the city remained embalmed.
You could walk the length of a boulevard
and never glimpse a crack in the wall of obedience.

Yet in the radio's thin static
I heard names breathed like passwords,
rumors of ground shifting far away.
Classmates whispered of fathers
taken in the night.
Fear rose sharp and fresh—
then turned into hunger.
Maybe the next broadcast would be the one.
Maybe the spark was already on its way.

      Teachers asked why I looked so close to anger,
told me to smile for the class picture.
But the smile they wanted belonged to another girl,
the one from before the waiting.

      I did what I could:
studied the core,
passed the rest,
and in the honest quiet after the slap,
saw my house again—
Mama's precision,
Clara's vigilance,
the way we breathed around each other
to keep the flame alive.
I had been drifting so far into contempt
that I'd stopped seeing the two people
holding the roof up.

      And so I kept to my radio—
by day, when the power allowed.
Not always for long,

but long enough to catch the tremors.
Long enough to believe something was moving toward us.

The country was holding its breath.
So was I.

When the winter of 1989 arrived,
the waiting had become a drumbeat in my chest.
And though the streets lay silent as a grave,
I was awake again—
cheek stinging,
eyes open—
watching my family,
watching the horizon,
ready.

~ ~ ~ ~ ~ ✧ ~ ~ ~ ~ ~

What Life Whispered to Me

Waiting can be its own kind of prison —
not built with walls or locks,
but with the bars of your own chest.

I learned that fear, carried too long,
hardens into something else.
It becomes impatience.
Fire.
The aching hunger for a moment
that hasn't yet come.

Hope isn't always light and pretty.
Sometimes it is heavy,
exhausting,
and tastes like iron in your mouth.
Sometimes it keeps you awake
long after midnight.

But even in stillness, there is movement.
Even in silence, the ground may already be shifting
beneath your feet.

I learned this not only from the radio,
but from the sting of a slap —
one that stripped away my arrogance

and forced me to see myself clearly.
In that moment, I understood:
sometimes the sharpest pain
is the very thing that wakes you up,
the line you must step over
to keep from losing yourself.

The waiting —
as unbearable as it feels —
is often the last deep breath
before everything changes.

Life whispered to me then:
There are seasons when you are not meant to run
ahead,
nor to turn away —
but to stand in the ache,
to feel the full weight of what you long for.

Because when the moment finally comes —
whether in the streets of a country
or in the heart of a single girl —
you will know exactly why you endured.

— Sophy Le'coa

~ ~ ~ ~ ~ ✧ ~ ~ ~ ~ ~

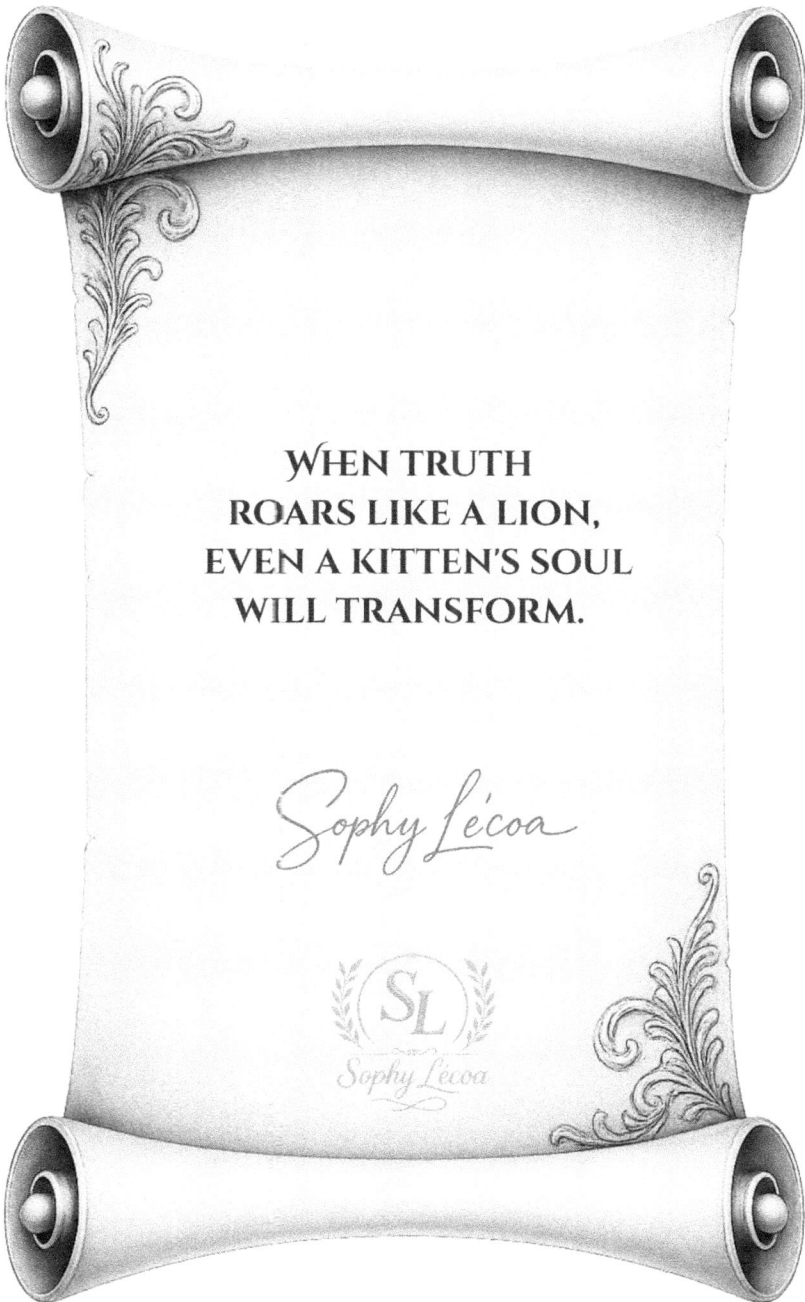

WHEN TRUTH
ROARS LIKE A LION,
EVEN A KITTEN'S SOUL
WILL TRANSFORM.

Sophy Lécoa

Chapter 29

The First Sparks

By the first bite of winter in 1989, the whispers we once chased under blankets changed shape.

They weren't rumors anymore.

They weren't guesses passed from one cautious neighbor to another.

They were headlines.

The Voice of America's signal cut sharper than ever before, slicing through the static with a clarity that left no room for doubt:

"Something big is coming. A movement. A plan. A revolution."

Clara and I locked eyes — wide, breathless — as though if we looked away, the moment itself might vanish. The change we had only dared to dream about, the one hidden behind silence and fear, was pressing at the door.

We were electrified — giddy, terrified, alive in a way we had never been before. Somewhere deep inside, I felt it: the days ahead would demand everything from us, and nothing would remain untouched.

Then, just weeks later, the impossible happened.

The television — usually a gray parade of propaganda — showed a live broadcast: the *Beloved Leader*, stiff on the balcony of the Presidential Palace. Same gray suit. Same frozen porcelain smile. Same mechanical wave over the obedient sea of faces.

We had seen this scene hundreds of times. The crowd was always silent, perfectly rehearsed in loyalty.

But this time… they weren't.

He began his speech, voice heavy with promises: more bread, more light, a brighter future under the Party's banner.

And then it happened.

The sound.

A noise I had never heard before in my life — not on television, not in the streets, not even whispered in secret.

Booing.

Not a slip. Not one voice.

A storm of voices. A roar — raw, unrestrained, undeniable.

Clara's hand gripped mine. My breath caught. Never, not once in our lives, had we heard this. Outrage, in daylight, in front of the world.

And what shook me more was his face.

He kept smiling. Kept gesturing. Kept talking, as if revolt itself hadn't risen beneath his balcony.

But I knew.

We both knew.

Something had cracked. And there was no going back.

The cameras jolted as the crowd surged, breaking barricades. Security rushed him inside. Later, we would learn the orders given in that sealed room:

Stop the protesters — by any means necessary.

Tanks rolled in. Soldiers were told to fire.

And then — the apartment door burst open.

Mama stood there, framed by the December wind, her coat smelling faintly of antiseptic, her hair swept back, her eyes blazing with urgency.

"Mama, you're home!" I ran to her. Clara was right behind me. We clung to her waist, hearts pounding.

She hadn't even set her bag down when the phone rang. She lifted the receiver. A voice barked orders — sharp, commanding, too loud. Her hand trembled once, but her face stayed still.

"Yes, Sir. I understand."

She placed the receiver down with quiet finality.

"I have to go back to the hospital. They've declared a national state of emergency. I don't know when I'll be back. You won't be able to reach me."

Her voice was calm, but its weight twisted my stomach.

Outside, the city unraveled — shouts, running feet, the crack of gunfire. The Revolution had begun, and Mama was stepping into the heart of it.

Clara and I stood frozen as she reached for her scarf. My hands shook as I grabbed the thicker one for her. Clara pressed a thermos of tea into her hands. We tried to help, but deep down we knew nothing could stop her.

Tears blurred my vision.

"No, Mama… please don't go."

"How will you even get there?" Clara whispered.

"I will get there," Mama said simply. "And I will come back."

She kissed our foreheads, sealing her words like a promise. Then she turned to the door.

Just before leaving, she looked back.

"Clara, take care of Sophy."

Her footsteps echoed down the stairwell. And as the sound faded, her voice floated upward — low, aching, sacred:

"Dear God… please help us."

We stood in the doorway, listening until she disappeared into the chaos.

The silence that followed was louder than the gunfire.

Clara whispered, "She's strong."

"But this is war," I said.

We didn't speak again. We didn't need to. We were holding onto the same fragile thread:

Her promise.

She would come back.

~ ~ ~ ~ ~ ✧ ~ ~ ~ ~ ~

What Life Whispered to Me

There are moments when the ground shifts beneath your feet, when fear climbs into your chest and steals your breath. But there are people who, when faced with the impossible, choose something else — not panic, not retreat, but resolve.

That day, Mama wasn't only our mother. She was a storm in motion, walking into danger with purpose, not desperation. She didn't plead with Heaven — she declared her place in the story:

"My children still need me — and this story is not over."

I saw her go not just as her daughter but as a witness — to the moment she crossed from the life we knew into the unknown, carrying only courage and faith.

I understood then: sometimes destiny isn't written in stars but spoken in a choice — a cry to the Universe that says:

I choose to rise.
I choose to live.
I choose to be.

Life whispered to me then:
If you dare to rise — even trembling, even afraid —
you can change everything.
For yourself.
For the ones you love.
For all that is still to come.

And though we didn't know it yet, the next time the door would open, it would not just be Mama returning — it would be the country itself, stepping back into the light.

— Sophy Le'coa

~ ~ ~ ~ ~ ✧ ~ ~ ~ ~ ~

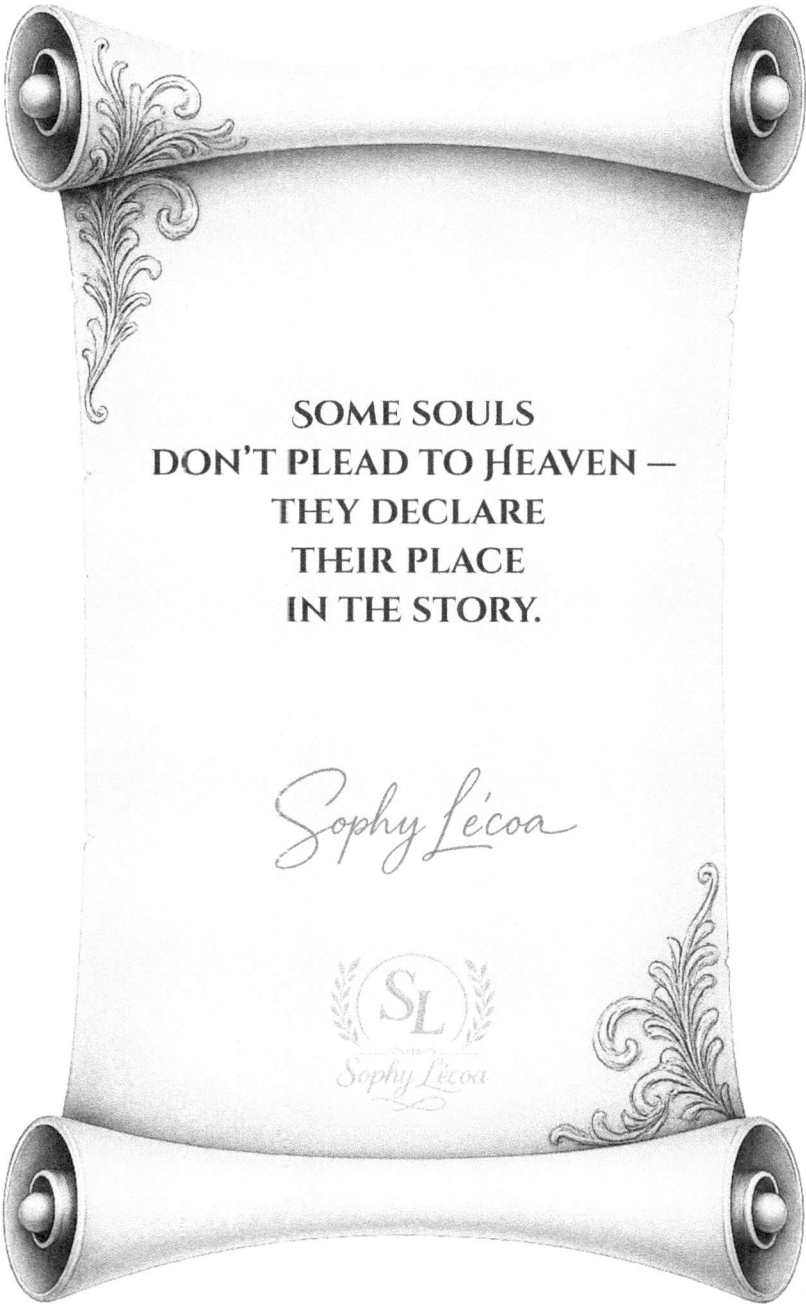

SOME SOULS
DON'T PLEAD TO HEAVEN —
THEY DECLARE
THEIR PLACE
IN THE STORY.

Sophy Lécoa

Chapter 30

The Last Communist Christmas

There were only three days left until Christmas when the first gunshots split the air.

No carols.

No cinnamon, no baking bread drifting from kitchens.

Only the sharp crack of bullets… and the metallic tang of fear, settling over the city like frost.

Mama was still at the hospital.

No calls.

No messages.

No word of life.

Only silence — that terrifying, echoing silence that wraps itself around your chest until you can barely breathe.

Clara and I clung to each other in those nights that felt like years.

We lay under the covers, fingers entwined, straining for any sound — a knock at the door, a familiar voice, a signal she was safe.

But nothing came.

Only the endless hum of the state-controlled television:

"The revolt will be suppressed."

"Order will be restored."

"The people have been manipulated."

We knew better.

Outside, the air itself felt charged — like the pause before lightning.

Whispers were moving.

People were rising.

And everyone knew: something was coming.

The only question was — would we live to see it?

Those were the longest three days of my life.

No decorations.

No joy.

Just shallow breaths, silent prayers, fear as heavy as winter itself.

And then... Christmas Day.

The television flickered.

The screen went black.

Clara and I stared, hardly daring to blink.

When the picture returned, it wasn't the face of the regime.

It was a group of young people — ragged, sleepless, eyes shining with something between exhaustion and triumph.

One of them stepped forward, voice trembling but unbroken:

"The Romanian people are free! The army is with us. We have won!"

For a moment, we were frozen.

Then it hit.

Clara burst into tears.

I shook from head to toe.

Was it real?

Was this hope — or some cruel trick?

And then came the images:

The dictator and his wife.

Fleeing by helicopter.

Captured.

Tried.

Executed.

Forty-five years of silence ended in one sentence:

România este liberă.

Romania is free.

The country erupted.

On every street corner, people wept and embraced strangers.

From every home, voices poured out of windows.

On every screen, banners blazed:

Un Craciun fara Nebun! (A Christmas without the Madman)
Un An Nou fara Tablou! (A New Year without the Portrait)

And just when my heart felt it could bear no more, we heard the key in the lock.

Mama.

She stood in the doorway, shoulders slumped from exhaustion, her coat carrying the bite of December air — but her eyes... her eyes were alive.

Tears welled as she whispered, almost to herself:

"It's over."

We ran.

We collided into her arms, sobs shaking us apart and binding us together all at once.

She held us so tightly I could barely breathe — and I didn't care.

Because she was here.

Because we were whole.

Because, against everything, she had come back.

Clara's voice cracked between tears.

"Sophy... you'll have bananas now."

I laughed and cried at once, the sound breaking in my throat.

To anyone else, it might have sounded silly.

But to us, it meant everything.

It meant choice.

It meant joy.

It meant a life where even fruit could no longer be forbidden.

That Christmas, there were no gifts under the tree.

No lights.

No carols.

No sweet bread in the oven.

What we had was greater.

We had freedom.

We had hope.

And we had Mama — home.

And in the deepest part of me, I knew: this was what the long waiting had been for. The whispers from the radio, the restless ache, the stubborn hope... all of it had been leading here.

It was the Christmas we became free — and I would carry its light forever.

"The joy of expressing freedom
is more than liberating —
it is divine."
— Sophy Le'coa

~ ~ ~ ~ ~ ✦ ~ ~ ~ ~ ~

What Life Whispered to Me

Sometimes the greatest miracles do not come wrapped in ribbons.
They arrive in silence.
In fear.
In longing.

And then, all at once — in freedom.

I learned that even when everything feels lost, light can break through in the most unexpected places.
That the pain of a nation can be washed clean by the courage of those who refuse to bow to fear.

That Christmas was not about receiving.
It was about returning — to life, to love, to a world remade.

For the first time, I felt it in my bones:
We were not just witnesses to history.
We were living it.

And maybe, one day,

I will tell the story to my kids and grandkids.

I understood then, Freedom, is never simply given.
It is earned.
It is fought for.
It is dreamed into being.

— *Sophy Le'coa*

~ ~ ~ ~ ~ ✧ ~ ~ ~ ~ ~

THE GREATEST
CHRISTMAS GIFT
IS REJOICING
IN GOD'S
GIFT OF FREEDOM.

Sophy Lécoa

Chapter 31

Born to Break the Spell

I used to think freedom came like fireworks —
loud, dazzling, impossible to ignore.

But the truth is, the spell didn't shatter in one grand
 explosion.
It unraveled in threads.

It began the day I chose to keep listening when I was
told not to.
It deepened when I dared to dream bigger than I was "
allowed."
It strengthened when I learned to carry love into places where
it had been rationed.

The spell had been woven from silence, fear, scarcity,
and the rules of other people's truths.
It told me to stay small.
To speak only when safe.

To believe that the life I saw in my mind's eye was too far away to touch.

But the girl I was —
the one who kept smiling in the dark —
refused to disappear.
Even when I didn't yet know her name, she lived inside me, waiting.

And with time, I learned one of life's most dangerous and beautiful skills:
Not to stop at the "truth" I was told.
To test it in my own hands.
To see if it held weight.
And when I found it — to trust it.
And when I trusted it — to stand in it, even if I stood alone.

I have met that girl now.
We've looked at each other in the mirror.
We've forgiven each other for all the times we had to hide.
And now, we walk forward together.

Breaking the spell isn't one single act.
It's choosing, again and again, to stay awake.
It's refusing to let the past become a cage — even when the door is open.
It's turning toward the life you were meant to live… and then living it, without apology.

If you've read this far, maybe you know your own spell.
Maybe you've been carrying it for years.

I can't break it for you.
But I can tell you this:

You are not alone in the dark.

And the light is not as far away as it feels.

We are all born to break the spell.

But we must choose — with every breath — to seek the truth for ourselves,

and to have the courage to believe it.

What Life Whispered to Me

I learned not to stop at what others called truth.

Instead, I followed my own trail —
reading between the lines,
uncovering what was hidden in plain sight.

It became second nature,
a quiet instinct to keep searching,
nose to the ground like a hound
on the scent of something rare and real.

I never let go, because each step deeper
only brings the joy of knowing:

the truth… never ends.

— Sophy Le'coa

~ ~ ~ ~ ~ ✧ ~ ~ ~ ~ ~

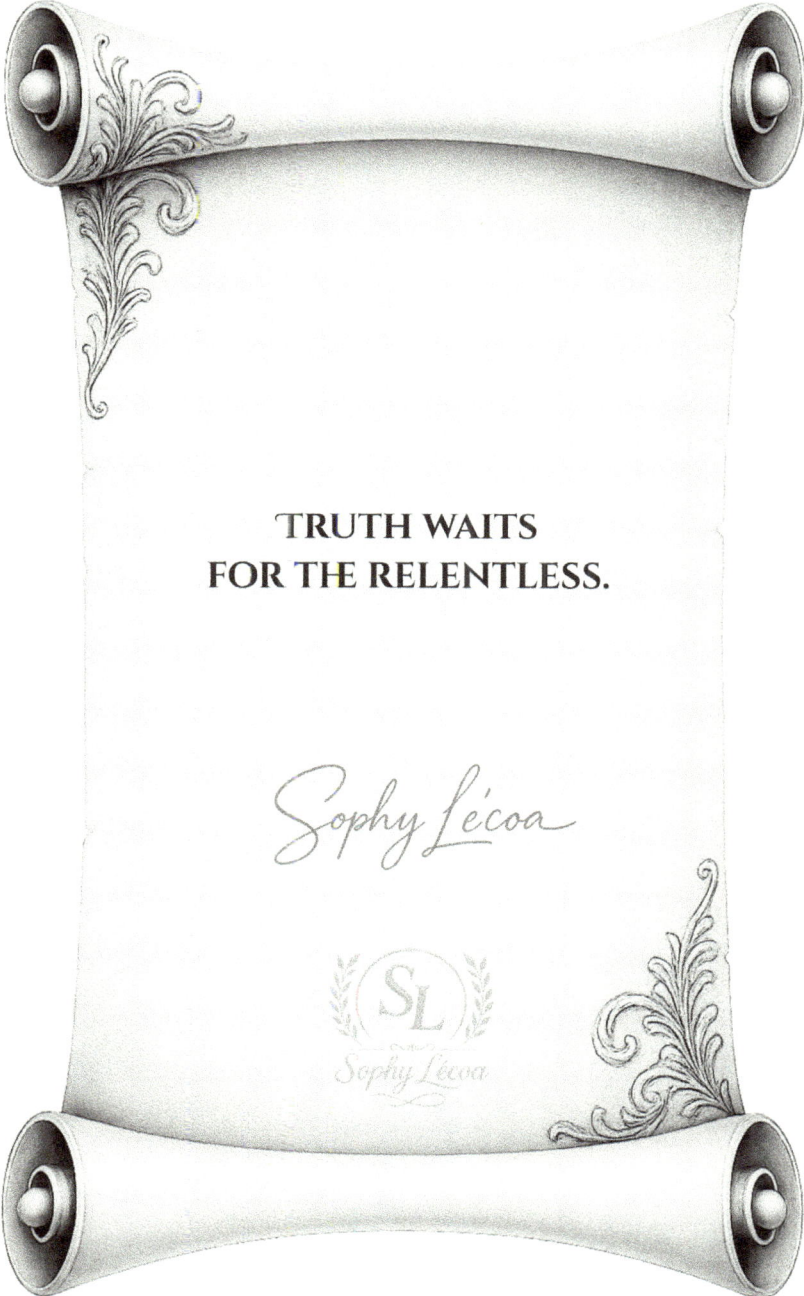

**TRUTH WAITS
FOR THE RELENTLESS.**

Sophy Lécoa

Epilogue

And now

When I look back, I see a little girl with ink-stained fingers, hiding by a radio, clinging to a smile that hid her cracks.

I see her running through gray streets, carrying hope she didn't know how to name.

I see her standing at the edge of shame in a classroom, a sting on her cheek, and learning that even pain can wake you up.

And I see her walking through the silence of communism — waiting, listening, believing — until the day the silence broke.

That girl was me.

And she is still with me.

Today, I live in a world she once only dreamed of.

A world where voices are free, where choices are mine, where truth isn't rationed but overflowing.

And still, every day, I choose to break the spell again.

Because freedom isn't a finish line — *it's a practice.*

Because courage isn't born once — *it must be carried.*

Because truth isn't something we inherit — it's something we search for, and *protect.*

And so I write these words for her — the girl who refused to disappear.

And I write them for you — so you know you are not alone.

The spell can be broken.

The truth can be found.

And the life waiting for you is closer than you think.

And yet, this is not the end.

The child who whispered through silence grew into a woman who kept walking, kept searching, kept breaking new spells.

Her story does not stop here — and neither does mine.

In the pages to come, I will open another chapter of this journey: one that carries the echoes of the past into the light of new beginnings.

So, when you close this book, don't close the story.

Because another one is already waiting for you.

✦ ✦ ✦

Author Note

This book was born from silence.
From rooms where laughter was hushed.
From moments when truth was too dangerous to speak.
From memories that pressed against my soul until I could no longer keep them hidden.

I wrote these pages because stories—especially the hard ones—deserve a voice. They are not only fragments of the past; they are living reminders that resilience can grow in shadows, that hope refuses to be erased, and that love can survive even the harshest winters of life.

What you've read here is not only my childhood. It is also the echo of countless lives shaped under the same sky, the same silence, the same unspoken dreams. The details may be mine, but the longings, the questions, the courage—they belong to us all.

If, while turning these pages, you found pieces of your own heart mirrored here, then the silence has been broken twice: once for me, and once for you.

Thank you for listening to the voice I once thought no one would hear.
Thank you for carrying these whispers forward.

With sincerity and fire,
Sophy Le'coa

Final Note

There are lives that begin in shades of gray —
days heavy, skies muted, dreams whispered so quietly they
almost vanish.
Mine began that way.

But even in the gray, there was light.
It came in small sparks — in forbidden laughter, in unexpected kindness, in fleeting colors that felt like miracles.

Page by page, year by year, those sparks gathered.
They grew into a fire I didn't yet know was inside me — a will
to see more, to be more, to live beyond what I was told was
possible.

And now, looking back, I know the truth:
The gray was never the end.
It was the beginning — the backdrop that made the colors
impossible to ignore when they finally came.

To every reader holding this book:
May you find the sparks in your own gray.
May you hold them until they multiply into something
brighter than you ever imagined.
And may you never forget — even the dullest beginnings can
bloom into the most vibrant stories.

From my heart to yours,
Sophy Le'coa

Why I Wrote This Book

For most of my life, my story lived in silence. Not because it wasn't worth telling, but because life had taught me to keep certain truths tucked away — safe from misunderstanding, safe from judgment, safe from the noise.

But years have a way of whispering. Moments I thought had faded returned, not as wounds but as teachers. The quiet child I once was — the one who watched the world with wide, wondering eyes — kept tugging at me. She wanted to be heard. She wanted her truth to breathe.

I finally understood I am not a human searching for a spirit.

I am spirit, living a human experience.

And this experience — mine — is not just my own. It belongs to every soul who has ever felt unseen, unheard, or misunderstood… yet kept moving toward the light.

I wrote this book because I believe every story, when told with truth and heart, can become a bridge — connecting not only past to present, but soul to soul.

I wrote it because silence, when carried too long, becomes a prison. And I was ready to step free.

This is not only the story of my childhood — it is a journey of awakening. Of remembering that we are far more than what we've been told. Of breaking free from the scripts handed to us and daring to write our own.

I wrote this book for the little girl I once was, for the woman I became, and for the spirit that has always been — unbroken, eternal, and free.

I wrote it for you, too. Because beneath all the differences, I believe we are the same:

spirits learning, growing, and remembering who we truly are.

I know now — we are not what we do or what we have.

We are that unique, pure spirit — manifested in a body meant to live a divine experience on Earth.

But because we've been taught to value what lies outside that truth, we judge others through the lens of illusion.

If we could all remember who we truly are, Earth itself could become Heaven.

About The Author

Sophy Lecoa was born in Brașov, Transylvania — in the heart of Romania, where every mountain, cathedral, and cobblestone carries a story. Just miles away stood the famed castle of Vlad Țepeș, the historical figure who inspired the Dracula legend, a reminder that history is never only myth but flesh, struggle, and memory.

Growing up under communism, Sophy's earliest years were marked by silence, scarcity, and resilience. It was from that silence she grew a voice — one that now stirs readers to tears, laughter, and revelation.

Sophy has traveled the world in search of meaning and truth, while sharpening her professional skills in the beauty industry. Though she has seen many countries, her heart still finds America the most beautiful place of all.

Today, Sophy lives in America, where she continues her journey as a writer and student of metaphysics. She is currently studying at the University of Metaphysics in Sedona, Arizona, and works in the beauty industry, where her clients often leave with more than style — they carry away words that stay with them for weeks, sometimes transforming long after they leave her chair.

With her debut memoir Born to Break the Spell, Sophy introduces not just her story, but her original voice — a style as sharp, playful, and "twisty" as it is profound, pressing on old certainties until they crack open to reveal a greater truth.

✦ ✦ ✦

"RESILIENCE IS NOT THE
ABSENCE OF WOUNDS,
BUT THE COURAGE TO TURN
THEM INTO WINGS.
IT IS THE QUIET FORCE THAT
CARRIES US
FROM BROKENNESS TO
BECOMING."

—Sophy Lécoa

www.ingramcontent.com/pod-product-compliance
Lightning Source LLC
Chambersburg PA
CBHW020149090426
42734CB00008B/760